THE RAY HARM NATURE SKETCHBOOK

THE RAY HARM

NATURE SKETCHBOOK

written and illustrated by RAY HARM

THE WORLD PUBLISHING COMPANY · CLEVELAND AND NEW YORK

Dedicated to Wood Hannah, Sr.

Published by The World Publishing Company
2231 West 110th Street, Cleveland, Ohio 44102

Published simultaneously in Canada by Nelson, Foster & Scott Ltd.

First Printing 1967

Library of Congress Catalog Card Number: 67–22914

PRINTED IN THE UNITED STATES OF AMERICA

CONTENTS

ꕥ·AUTUMN

ꕥ·WINTER

I · SPRING

✐·Isolation in the Woods?

Spring is the season of new life, and although autumn may be the most breath-taking season to behold, spring is undoubtedly the most welcome. Things in nature are growing rapidly; the winter deep-sleepers emerge to life again; much of the life that went to sleep in one form last fall is awakening in a totally changed form of life.

One spring morning, the mourning-cloak butterfly, the question-mark, and zebra swallowtail were about, silently flitting to early flowers in bloom. The zebras at one place were congregated along the edge of a shallow puddle of water, pulsing their wings open and closed. (A variety of butterflies often collect at the flowing sap of a tree where the sapsucker has been working. This creates a remarkable bouquet of living color.) The chorus frogs, and spring peepers and toads filled the air with a profusion of voice.

April is the time when the hepatica, bloodroot, twinleaf, pepperroot, salt and pepper, bittercress, and Dutchman's breeches around the house are in full bloom. The columbine, red trillium, and bluebells will soon open. Leatherwood is in its yellow bloom, and the spicebush is chartreuse green on the hillsides; the willows repeat this on the creek and river bottoms. I noticed that on the hornbeams and hazelnuts the catkins are thick and swelling.

With each sunny day more and more lizards are scampering over leaves, fallen logs, and up tree trunks. I found a nest of flying squirrels in the top of a broken beech trunk and climbed a tree alongside to look in on them. The adult squirrel exploded straight up and glided to safety some thirty yards down the hollow. Startled aplenty and feeling a little guilty about poking my nose into the nest, I quickly left, hoping the disturbed parent would return, none the worse for the scare.

Vultures returned by the hundreds throughout February and March. One night, 173 turkey vultures roosted in two or three large white oak trees across the lake and hollow from our house near Bernheim Forest. The next day these, as other recent flocks, went on their way, circling westward.

On March 16, near suppertime, a long line of whistling swans, flying abreast (also headed west), flew low over the house, sending down their great babbling chatter as they passed. I counted sixty-two of them. Gadwall ducks and scaups, mallards, blacks, grebes, wood ducks, and coots have stopped to rest on our lake.

I first heard phoebes singing this year on March 14 but could barely hear their voices because of a flock of about thirty purple finches scattered in the trees around, singing loudly. These melodious voiced, raspberry-colored birds spent the winter with us, and at this writing they are still present. The white-eyed vireo is back from the Gulf Coast and is joined in chorus by many of the permanently resident birds who are now singing in earnest.

Yes, spring is the season of life and activity. I laugh when people remark how isolated I am "out in the sticks."

Butterflies. Upper left: question-mark; lower center: mourning-cloak; others: zebra swallowtails

3

Whippoorwill. Inset: right foot

4

·Seldom-Seen Whippoorwill on the Fly

If I had to live in an area where whippoorwills were not found, it would surely leave some empty spots in my spring and summer nights. We first heard their calls this spring on April 12, in the hollow where we live. Every evening for two weeks after, new ones joined in, until their voices completely dominated the evening. The whippoorwill is probably heard more and seen less than any other bird in our section of the country.

Once started, it often calls incessantly. On nights spent in the woods, I have drowsed off to sleep after counting more than a thousand successive calls from an individual bird.

The whippoorwill is not easily seen in the daytime, devoting most of its active time to the nights. While walking in the woods, I occasionally flush up a whippoorwill from under a fallen tree, and it never fails to impress me with its noiseless flight. Its spotty, wavy-barred coloration is such that it is difficult to see it against the forest floor where it spends the daytime.

This bird has an unusually large mouth which serves as a scoop when gathering insects in flight. Above each edge of the upper bill grows a row of long, very stiff, hairlike bristles called rictal bristles, which act as "feelers," and a "scoop" that aids the bird in catching flying insects.

Sometimes, whippoorwills fly very close to our house at night catching beetles, moths, and other insects that are attracted by the lights inside. The birds are like large moths themselves as they dart about silently.

They build no nest; the female lays her blotched, white eggs right on the leaves or bare ground and, although the young are born more fully developed than many other birds, they nevertheless need constant care from the mother bird for awhile.

Much has been written in the past about the alleged ability of whippoorwills and chuck-will's-widow (a close relative) in times of danger to carry away their eggs in their large mouths to a safer place. Unfortunately, this story has been picked up by nature writers and carried on for many years without any real basis in reputable observations.

The feet of these birds are of particular interest, being very small and undeveloped for the size of the body because the whippoorwill is neither a perching nor walking bird. It spends most of its nonhunting time on the ground. The middle toe has a peculiar claw (see inset), curved and finely toothed. Since the bird spends so much time on the forest floor and consequently is exposed to many insects, this claw is perfect for "combing" insects from its plumage.

·Flickers' Courting Ceremony

One April morning, my field studies were interrupted by a group of amorous flickers who flew to a branch just above me. Naturally, I

Flickers. Female at left; others are male

6

took advantage of their antics and recorded them with sketches from which this drawing was made.

The courtship ceremonies of these woodpeckers are fascinating to watch. They go through a variety of stretches, bows, wing and tail spreading, and other postures to win the affections of a mate.

This picture was sketched during a frozen position, held by all four birds for about ten seconds. The two birds on the left were the first to fly to the branch and face each other. Immediately, they spread their tails to the maximum, exposing a fan of beautiful mustard color underneath. With their tails held in the fanned position, they both began a slow back-and-forth swaying from side to side, each in the opposite direction, all the while making jerky movements with their heads. At the peak of one of these sideward movements, they often froze for varying intervals of time, as in the drawing.

Notice that the bird on the left has no black "whisker" marking on the face. The absence of this mark identifies her as the female bird. This mark evidently plays an important part in recognition for the courtship of the flicker.

After some five minutes of this courtship, the two were joined in rapid succession by two more males, who alighted on the same branch. At first, the third bird also faced the female bird from behind the first male, but, when the fourth bird landed, he turned around to face him. The two pairs together then went into the same courtship displays.

The whisker-marked birds are the males and probably the reason the last two males were "courting each other" was because of the presence of the female. I suppose that the male on the end was looking past the other two males and was being triggered to display by the sight of the female. Bird number three, facing him but originally aware of the presence of the female, was duped momentarily by this courting action and reacted with the same display.

Not for long, though, because after a few minutes the first pair flew away. This stopped the action momentarily. Then the last male started to display again but got no reaction from the other remaining bird so he, too, flew away.

Birds have a variety of displays. Some, like the mating displays in this instance, are very beautiful, with use of their crests, open wings and tails, and strange stance. Other displays express different meanings—hostility, distraction, defense, and so on—all most interesting to observe.

✐·Singing Stakes Out Nesting Claim

Birds are most distinguishable from other animals by their ability to fly, and probably next noted for their ability to sing. And what purposes do the vocal efforts of birds really serve?

Bird songs do have a definite purpose, and with most species the song itself is performed only during part of the year, although some birds will sing more or less throughout the year.

Birds in my part of the country, Kentucky,

Kentucky warbler singing

sing in the spring and early summer. These songs are usually sung to attract a mate and to establish a nesting territory, the latter being the most common reason. This proclaims to all other males the singer's ownership of nesting territory, and he will fight to defend it.

Most birds sing in early morning or late afternoon, but some sing at the oddest hours, even all through the night, as does our mockingbird sometimes. Some birds will cease singing after they have chosen a mate, and most of them stop entirely during the period of feather molting.

There is much variation of song in different birds of the same species. The Kentucky cardinal has more than two dozen distinct song variations, but the quality of each is typically the cardinal voice. The female cardinal sings quite as well and sometimes better than the male.

The mockingbird, catbird, and thrasher are our "mimics," but there are several other birds that also imitate, the starling, for example. And I have been fooled many times by the similarity of a call of the bluejay to that of the redshouldered hawk.

There are several types of bird songs. There are "flight songs" that birds such as the goldfinch, snipe, horned lark, and the purple finch sing while flying, but most birds do not sing in flight. There are the "call notes" which apply to many different things—a signal to communicate among themselves, a warning note, or a threat.

There is also a type of quiet song I have heard many birds sing when I was close to them. It is the same major song they sing aloud, but barely audible. They sing it almost under their breath. One of the most beautiful songs I have heard in this manner is that of the handsome rose-breasted grosbeak.

Some birds—the pelican is one—have no voice at all; and the large turkey vulture I see so frequently above my section of the country is capable of emitting only guttural noises and grunts.

When it comes to judging bird songs esthetically, I have some favorites; not always because of tonal quality, but because of my association with the birds themselves. To name a few, the "common ole song sparrow," the Carolina wren, the whippoorwill, the cuckoo, and the clucking of a pileated woodpecker really get to me. So does the voice of the veery. I like to hear a bluebird just to know he's around.

Actually, all bird voices rate pretty highly with me—the woods wouldn't be the same without them.

·Nests Are for Hatching Young

For a long time, the little house wren has been a favorite of many people because of its willingness, like that of bluebirds in the past, to take up housekeeping so close to man.

Wrens prefer cultivated areas, free of undergrowth, such as those areas created by home landscaping. They are insect eaters, and with insect controls so heavily employed these days around homes, it is not unlikely that many wrens have fallen victims to the poisons or have vacated their nests because of the lack of insects to feed their young.

These small birds are exceptionally active, almost nervously so. Their tails are carried characteristically high, sometimes cocked up over their backs almost pointing at their heads.

Wrens are well-known for their unusual nesting spots. I have known them to build in tin cans, pots, old tires, pockets in coats hanging in garages, and old felt-hat crowns, to name a few. Willingly, they accept man's habitat.

Bird-nest locations are interesting, but I sometimes wonder how much, if any, intelligence is reflected in the bird's selection of a place, including even the more complex nests and locations. The more I study birds, the more I am aware of how strongly they are motivated by instinct. For example, an indigo bunting builds a perfect indigo-bunting nest the first time, just as its parents before it, using the same type of materials, construction, and location without ever having seen it done before.

Birds do not use their nests for homes. They do not use them to sleep in at night or for spending idle hours. And few birds use the same nest more than once. The purpose for which a bird builds a nest is solely the raising of its young.

Birds such as whippoorwills, woodcocks, and killdeers lay their eggs directly on the ground, which seemingly would provide little protection. The eggs and the incubating adult, however, are extremely well camouflaged, difficult to see even at close range—another example of "survival of the fittest." Tree nests are generally safer than ground nests, but are not as safe as nests built in tree trunks, such as the holes woodpeckers make.

Wrens will nest in almost any cavity avail-

House wren

able. Often, if there are several cavities within the vicinity of the nest, they are soon filled with sticks, creating false nests to further "stake their claim" to that territory.

·See the "Butterflies of the Bird World"

Warblers are tiny birds. About five inches in length, they offer the greatest challenge to "birders" (as people who watch birds like to call themselves). Few nonbirders are actually aware of these little birds and, when they see warblers for the first time, are greatly surprised that such birds exist "in these parts." Often referred to as "butterflies of the bird world," different species of warblers display a great array of intensely beautiful color and pattern variation.

Spring is the big season to observe the greatest variety of warblers because of the mass migration of the many species from southern parts to northern nesting grounds during that time. It is the best time to see them because these birds are then found in their brilliant spring breeding colors, the easiest to learn.

Fall becomes a much more difficult season in which to recognize the same birds; on their return trip south many have changed their plumage to a dull green and yellow, one bird looking much like the next. It takes a good many years for the birder to learn the differences among the fall warblers.

Black and white warbler

11

Learning the bird's voice helps a good deal, and for those really interested in accepting the challenge of learning these "butterflies" there are a few additional aids for reducing the number of years sometimes required to learn them.

First, obtain a "checklist" to the warblers found in your area. Local bird clubs or natural history museums are very helpful; they usually list also the summer resident birds of the area. These lists will aid considerably by immediately eliminating many birds from your bird guide that would not be found in your locality, and enabling you first to learn the warblers that are local summer residents so that they can then be more easily distinguished from the transient arrivals next spring.

Try to learn the voices of the local summer residents as soon as possible. There is, of course, another helpful item—a pair of size 7 × 50 field glasses. Many prefer size 7 × 35, which has the same magnification and is a lighter pair of glasses, but it lets less light into the field of vision.

I have a great respect for birders; having worked with several groups over the years, I find them to be acutely observant and aware of the world around them. Most are seriously and scientifically interested in the behavior of our wildlife; they collectively provide our government with essential records of migrations, animal behaviors, nesting habits, and range limits for animals across our country. The federal wildlife people depend annually upon these records to provide the needed wildlife conservation methods for the future.

If you think that you are pretty observant and your memory is good, go out and start learning to identify the various birds you see and hear. You'll be surprised how little you've been aware of the common things in nature around you.

It will sharpen not only your memory and your physical senses, but also your sense of values.

Know Your Onions—and Your Mushrooms!

When spring is in full swing and new life is "busting out all over," those edible wild plants of the season, emerging once again, entice my family to get the baskets and head for the woods. The sight of redbud blossoms, cattail shoots, pokeberry, ramps, and mushrooms recalls many seasons of good eating for us.

Mushrooms are often ignored by people who are attracted to the outdoors. Even so, there are many strange and unusually colorful forms of fungi to be seen, and some are delicious to eat. But, caution! More people are killed in our country by mushroom poisoning than by rattlesnake bites (which really doesn't mean much, because the incidence of death due to snakebite is very low).

The various species of edible mushrooms, however, are sometimes quite difficult to distinguish from the poisonous species, of which many are *very* poisonous, so mushroom hunters

12

Mushrooms. Left: amanita (poisonous);
right: morel (edible)

13

must take care to recognize the good and the bad. Grave results may occur from an error in identification.

Even one poisonous mushroom in a basket of edible ones can "infect" them and make them poisonous. The trouble is that often, when the mushrooms are picked, many young poisonous ones are similar in appearance to the older edible ones. A good book on the subject is essential for the beginner mushroom seeker.

One group of mushrooms called the "amanitas" must be avoided. There are between twenty-five and thirty-five species of amanitas in the United States, and although a few of these are edible, *no* amanita should be eaten unless positively identified as an edible species. To attest to their toxicity, the amanitas have been given such names as "destroying angel," "death cup," "deadly amanita," "panther mushroom," and so on. These fungi are considered even more toxic when raw, and there is a case on record of a human death caused by eating only a third of a single cap of the amanita verna, the most widespread and common form of amanita.

I rarely eat any other than two species of mushrooms: the morel and the puffballs—both easily identified. Morels are sometimes called "sponge mushrooms" (see drawing). Puffballs will sometimes grow to weigh over five pounds; a lot of good eating there, and this mushroom is even good to eat raw in salads.

Morels are prepared by soaking them first in salt water overnight. Then rinse, slice, and roll the slices in cornmeal; brown them in butter in a saucepan. Try them.

14

Bittern Blends into Marsh

It was a warm spring day. As my wife Carmella and I drove along a blacktop country road, I spotted an American bittern (one of the marsh birds) ahead on the shoulder of the road. As I slowed down to get a good look at this interesting bird, it suddenly stood at attention, stretching its head and neck straight up with its bill pointed skyward. The bird held that position like a statue.

I stopped the car, then slowly got out and crossed the road. So confident was the bittern in its stance that it allowed me to come very close; so close that I eased my hand out and put my finger within an inch of its upward-pointed bill before it flew off.

In the marshes, I had seen this pose assumed many times by bitterns sensing danger, but there on the road it seemed out of place. I should never have expected to get that close to the bird anyplace. This was a good illustration of how a bird reacts by instinct instead of reason. Nature provides that this bird use instinct to escape detection; in this instance, however, the bittern actually made itself stand out like a sore thumb.

In its natural habitat of the marsh or swamp, the bittern is a marvel of protective coloration and habit. It moves stealthily among the reeds, marsh grasses, and cattails looking for food, and at the slightest sign of danger assumes this position, blending immediately into the vertical background growth. I have seen bitterns become even more effective with their camouflage

by actually swaying back and forth with the bending grasses and cattails.

This stance is so much a part of the bittern's life that, through evolution, it has developed eyes capable of seeing straight forward while its head is pointed skyward (see sketch). As if this were not enough to make the bird interesting, the sounds it makes are more remarkable. They have been likened to many things, and are hard to describe with words, but a comparison to the sound of an old-fashioned farm pump in action and the clack of a stake being driven fits as well as any.

The American bittern is not a small bird, standing easily two feet high when in the alert, protective stance. When its head is pulled in close to its body, it seems quite compact.

Marsh birds are entertaining to watch. They stalk their prey—fish, crayfish, frogs, and insects—with great skill. They are lightning fast in making their catch. Of course, Kentucky is not the land of the marsh; consequently, bitterns may be seen along the edge of farm ponds, rivers, and bogs and, during the migration periods in the spring, almost anyplace.

Tree Frog Adds to Night Song

Woodland voices can be quite deceiving. It is often difficult for the uninitiated to identify what species of animal makes which sound.

The chipmunk's "chipping," for example, is often mistaken for the note of the cardinal. The

American bittern

15

Tree frogs. Above: female; below: male

staccato voice of the very young raccoon is also perplexing when first heard; and even while watching a blue-winged warbler sing its song, the observer would swear an insect is making the sound. I know that when I am with anyone who is hearing his first woodchuck "whistle" he is at a complete loss trying to guess the source.

One of the most common voices of the springtime is that of the spring peeper, yet few people have actually seen one of these little tree frogs.

Only an inch long, this fellow and his many companions can fill the night completely with their calling. In addition, they usually share their puddle, pond, or bog with several other species of frogs and toads, all calling to attract a mate.

This tiny brown amphibian is marked very distinctively with an "X" on his back; I call it a "sign of the times." The ends of his toes are equipped with little discs which have a sticky substance. This enables the frog to climb almost like a fly on vertical and overhead surfaces.

I have often taken my family to the puddles and marshes after dark when the voices are full and, using flashlights, have enjoyed immensely the wholly different world out in the woods at night. If you are the inquisitive type, try the flashlight approach. (Daylight observation is possible but less successful.)

The frogs, toads, and nocturnal insects really put on a show. Strangely enough, the light does not seem to interfere with their activities, although the observer must be silent. The inflated vocal sacs are astonishing. Surely they should burst under such pressure, but they don't, and serve their purpose well by producing vocal sounds of unbelievable intensity.

The female peeper does not sing, but after she has been attracted by the voice of a male, and her eggs have been fertilized, she attaches them all (several hundred of them) to sticks and plant life below the surface of the water. These hatch into tadpoles which eventually become peepers (that is, those that are overlooked by fish, birds, and other animals that eat frogs' eggs and tadpoles).

After mating, spring peepers spend the rest of the summer up in the trees, feeding on insects. In less than two months the tadpoles become frogs and join the adults in the trees in a quiet life of hunting food.

When fall arrives, they all descend and bury themselves under the forest floor of leaves to spend the winter in hibernation until the next spring, when they emerge and the entire cycle is repeated.

✍·Box Turtle Is a Busy Fellow

Last year, on the top of Bearwallow Knob, above our home, I came upon an empty box turtle shell. It was upside down, stuck fast in the mud at the edge of a little pond there. Apparently the turtle had attempted to crawl over a log and slipped over backwards into the sticky mud, where it was held tightly until it died. A perfect skeleton told the story.

Locally, the box turtle is called "terrapin,"

although the names "turtle" and "terrapin" usually are applied to water turtles, which the box turtle is not, primarily. The name "tortoise" is more often applied to dry land turtles such as the tortoise of the West and Deep South.

By the third week of April this year, box turtles were out and on the move in great numbers, searching for mates. On one of my trips into the woods with my son Hap, we found no fewer than fifteen wandering males in three hours.

We lifted each one as we found it and identified it as male by examining the plastron (lower shell), which is concave, or dished. The females have a flat, or often a convex plastron. (We came upon some that had already found a mate and were busy getting acquainted. Our presence didn't seem to disturb them.)

Box turtles have beautiful markings which may be in colors ranging from bright orange or yellow to olive on a background of nearly black or brown. These colors may be over the entire turtle. The eyes of the males frequently are red, while the females usually have yellow or brown eyes.

The hard shell of the box turtle, like the specializations of the skunk and porcupine, enables it to roam the woods in comparative safety from predators. I have seen hungry foxes break through turtle shells, like a dog with a bone, but it is seldom that they are successful with a full-grown turtle.

The turtle's ability to close its shell very tightly, using a hinge on the bottom shell, offers great protection. It is comical to find a fat fellow who cannot quite contain himself. When picked up, an overly fed turtle will try to close his shell for protection, but finds he bulges out on both ends. If his tail end is touched he may manage to pull that end in tightly, but out pops the other end, and he finds he has literally eaten himself out of house and home.

Female box turtles lay their eggs in a hole which they dig for that purpose, then cover them with soil. The eggs hatch in late summer. After the newly hatched turtles dig themselves out, they try to keep hidden; they are vulnerable at this age. Much growing must take place before the shell hardens enough for protection. The hinge on the lower shell also needs a couple of years for development.

Throughout the winter the box turtles are dormant under the surface of the ground, where they have dug in to hibernate. Their body activities are greatly reduced at this time, but spring finds them digging out and wandering again, sometimes for miles, looking for another mate.

Box turtle

Purple Martin Pays His Rent

A good neighborhood insect control to have around the house is a bird called the purple martin. Martins have voracious appetites for insects, and one bird can consume thousands of them daily.

There are many interesting varieties and designs of martin houses made for attracting these swallows. Most are built by the home carpenter-hobbyist, and some are quite ornate, with decorative pillars, gables, fasciae, and cornices.

Designers of these large birdhouses have contrived ingenious methods for raising and lowering them for cleaning and storage, using counterbalances, levers, and the like.

It is not unusual for martin apartment houses to weigh up to two hundred pounds or more, and I have seen houses containing as many as thirty-six holes. Considering the number of insects consumed by a pair of martins in a day, that's a lot of local insect control.

Martin houses need not be elaborate, however —a colony can be attracted to a simple row or two of hollow gourds, with proper entrance holes cut out, attached to a horizontal pole. Such poles are frequently seen in the yards of rural homes in the South. Or, a wooden house containing only six or eight compartments can start a colony. Additional stories may be added later if more martins are desired.

Two or three things will help make a martin house successful: The apartments should be separate and about six inches square; the entrance holes should be two and a half inches in

Purple martin

19

diameter; the house itself should be erected on a pole between fifteen and twenty feet high.

Sparrows and starlings can be discouraged by keeping the entrances closed or covered until the martins are due to arrive. In Kentucky they can start arriving each spring around mid-March, but more frequently they come in late March or early April. A nesting martin will defend its territory from intruders once it has claimed an apartment.

✍·Many Factors Make Life Hard for Bluebirds

Several years ago, near my home, I watched a little house wren make many trips to a nearby bluebird-nesting hole, pull out the material brought there by that bird, and replace it with his own pile of sticks. Though he never used the site for nesting, he kept it full of his sticks and established it as his territory, fighting any bird that became interested in it.

A few seasons later I watched another wren break up the housekeeping of another pair of bluebirds by pulling the newly hatched young out of the nest and letting them drop to the ground.

The bluebird is scarce, and other things besides the house wren threaten its existence. The starling, the sparrow, and man's use of chemical insecticides all play important parts in its disappearance.

These other birds, which compete strongly with the bluebird for nesting space, are multi-plying rapidly as man provides more and more unnatural habitats in which they thrive. Eastern bluebirds nest in open areas—the edges of fields, in orchards, or near homes. With the increased use of insecticides by man, the birds have found little insect life (their primary food in the summer) on which to feed and have been victims of the poisons.

Various birds of the world have become symbols—the owl for wisdom, the peacock for pride, the ostrich for self-delusion, the dove for peace, and so on. Because the bluebird has long symbolized happiness by his color, song, and spring arrival, the bird is a favorite of man. (Remember the quest for happiness dramatized in Maeterlinck's *The Blue Bird?*) His red, white, and blue coloration has often made him a popular candidate for our national bird.

The adult birds usually return year after year to the same nesting place, where they may raise three broods in a season and, rarely, a young one from an earlier brood will help its parents feed new brothers and sisters in the same season. When the bluebirds flock together for the winter, however, the young ones forget family ties and in the spring find their own nesting areas. Occasionally, adults will change mates between broods during a season.

The erection of man-made bluebird houses has aided considerably in attracting these birds to areas where natural cavities such as woodpecker holes, hollow trees, or even rock crevices no longer exist. The bluebird is admired by so many that there have been concerted efforts nationally by organizations and individuals trying to save it by providing houses and habitat to encourage bluebird nesting.

Bluebird. Adult feeding grasshopper to young

21

Tulip tree blossom

Ray Harm

22

Kentucky's Popular Tulip Tree

The tallest tree in the eastern United States is the tulip tree, which approaches two hundred feet in height at full growth. This majestic giant of the forest has been selected as the state tree of three states: Kentucky, Tennessee, and Indiana.

It is commonly miscalled a "yellow poplar," or "tulip poplar," but it is, in fact, closely related to the magnolias and is not a poplar at all. I don't know whether the "yellow" part of its name refers to the color of the flower or of the heartwood; in either case, both are more green than yellow. Whether or not it was tagged "poplar" because of the softness of the wood or the rustling, poplar-like sound the leaves make in a breeze, I don't know either.

Moreover, I have worked with loggers in some sections of the country who refer to it by none of the above names but call it "whitewood" for its white, soft sapwood.

In spite of the softness of its wood, the tulip tree is classified a hardwood—which seems not to make sense, but trees with broad leaves are generally referred to by loggers and woodsmen as "hardwoods" and the evergreen trees as "softwoods," regardless of the grain texture of their wood. This tree does have a broad leaf which puts it into the general hardwood classification.

The wood of the tulip tree is fine for wood carving, being soft and easy to work. The first time I ever saw a froe and mallet used was on a section of the even-grained tulip tree. (A froe is a wedge-shaped cleaving blade with a right-angled handle, used to split shingles by hand.)

In the eastern part of our country, the tulip tree is valuable as a timber tree, used for such purposes as wall paneling, furniture, veneers; and it is even shredded for excelsior. Its ability to withstand warping puts it to use as drawer bottoms and wide floor boards. For my own home I chose half-logs of tulip tree to serve as stairs and the fireplace mantel. The handsome color of the greenish heartwood makes our stairway right nice to look at.

I am not aware that the tree grows west of the Mississippi to any great extent, but it is widespread in the East.

The bark of the young tulip tree is decidedly different in appearance from that of the older tree. It is smooth, with whitish lines spottily running vertically up the trunk. These lines remain as the bottom of the furrows that form in the bark as the tree matures. The very old trees have thick ridges of bark on the trunk that crowd the whitish lines from view.

The flower of the tulip tree, large as it is (as much as two inches deep and three to four inches across) is often missed by the casual observer because of the great heights this tree attains. I know that the honey made by bees from these large flowers in May and June tastes mighty good.

·Watch Pokeweed's Toxic Roots

Poke, pokeweed, pokeberry, pigeonberry, and scoke are a few local names for a well-known wild edible plant found in the eastern United States.

The roots of pokeweed are quite poisonous; hogs have been known to die from eating them. Some folks claim the berries, too, are poisonous, but I have tasted good pokeberry pie.

Perhaps cooking removes the toxic properties in the seeds (*if* they are toxic). I am reasonably sure that the pulp of the raw berry is safe, but I make no claims about the raw seeds, one way or the other.

I have watched birds consume large quantities and I know possums eat them, but birds swallow the seeds whole and a possum—well, a possum eats almost anything, anyway. Once it grows beyond the tender shoot stage in the spring, none of the plant should be eaten.

Carmella has an unhappiness with the brightly colored juice of the berries. A bird, after having consumed a quantity of them, can reduce a white sheet on the line to an artistic abstraction with one deposit.

The wild pokeweed plant sometimes grows to a height of nine feet and is easily identified by its thick, bright, magenta-colored stalk. In August, its glossy purple berries are unmistakable.

Pokeberry is eaten in several ways. The tender leaves and shoots are picked when four to six inches tall. These fresh, spring greens are boiled, the cooking water is discarded, and they are served as a vegetable with cream sauce.

In the South, the plant is cultivated as a garden green. One way to have fresh greens all winter long is to dig the large roots of pokeberry late in the autumn and plant them in

23

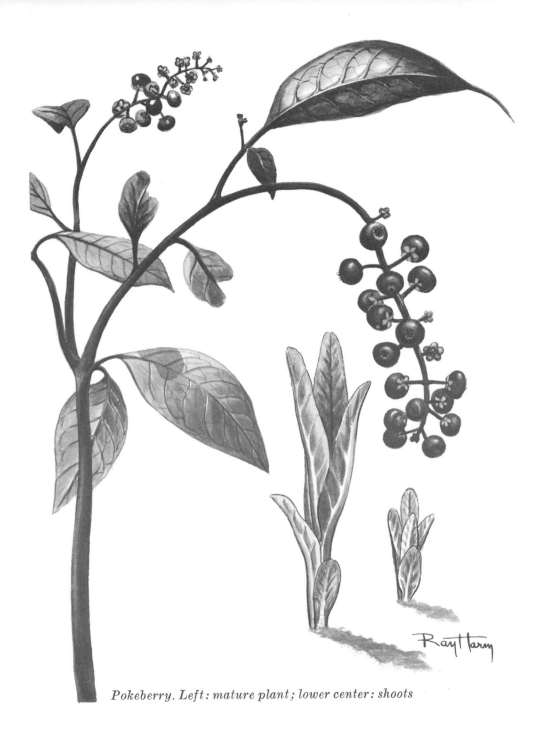

Pokeberry. Left: mature plant; lower center: shoots

suitable soil-filled wooden boxes in a dark corner of the basement. If they are watered regularly, there should be ample poke greens available to eat throughout the cold months. The leaves will emerge (crop after crop) yellowish green in color, and tender, and they should be cut for use when about six inches tall.

Buttered boiled poke shoots are good eating, too. The shoots should be soaked in salt water for an hour or so (as in the preparation of wild mushrooms), then drained and boiled in fresh water for a half hour or more. Salt to taste and melt butter over them.

Mountain people make pickles of poke greens by gathering the young plant in the wild while the shoots are still solid in the center. After removing the skin from the shoots, they are cut to the desired pickle length and placed in the canning jar.

Make the pickling liquid as follows: Mix 1 cup of sugar, 2 heaping teaspoons of salt, 1 teaspoon of whole cloves, 2 sticks of cinnamon, 1½ cups of vinegar, ½ cup of water. Boil this mixture for five to ten minutes and pour it over the pickle-sized poke shoots in the canning jar. Seal the jar, and that's it.

Warblers, a Rare Case of Crossbreeding

There is little interbreeding in wildlife, although hybridization does occur occasionally, more often in species that are not ''monogamous'' (that do not pair off for the season with one mate). Crossbreeding is most likely to occur where the breeding ranges of two closely related species overlap, such as the mallard duck and the black duck. These two ducks, in other than external markings, resemble each other very closely in size, habit, shape, and range.

When a hybrid is produced between two closely related species, the chances of its finding and mating with another hybrid are remote in the wild. Much more probably, it will mate with an individual of full strain; thus the dominant species maintains itself in strength.

In a rare case where a cross may occur between two more distantly related species, the offspring are usually not fertile. This situation can sometimes be completely reversed and controlled, however, under captive or domestic conditions.

Interspecies breeding, as uncommon as it is, is found with some frequency between two warblers called the golden-winged warbler and the blue-winged warbler. This interbreeding can occur where the geographical ranges of the two species overlap, but there seems to be no toleration between the two species within their private ranges.

There are two possible results from this crossing of the two warbler species. One hybrid, which resembles the golden-winged parent, is called the Lawrence's warbler; the other, which resembles the blue-winged parent, is called the Brewster's warbler. The hybrid Brewster's warbler is more common than the Lawrence's, suggesting that the blue-winged parent species

Warblers. Top: blue-winged; middle: golden-winged; bottom: Brewster's warbler

25

is genetically the stronger of the two. There are enough consistent differences in these hybrids that, for many years after they were first discovered, they were thought to be separate species.

It was a rare treat for me one April to show my wife a blue-winged, a golden-winged, and a Brewster's warbler all in the same tree, feeding on the flowers of a sugar maple that overhangs our sundeck. We were further delighted to hear all three sing at the sighting. The hybrid Brewster's warbler may have the voice of either parent. In this case it had that of the blue-winged, although it fell short of the full vocal development of a true blue-winged warbler.

This sighting was at the height of migration of birds coming in on their way north, and in the same tree were also a cerulean warbler, a prairie warbler, and hooded warblers, plus a summer tanager.

I have yet to see the other hybrid, the Lawrence's warbler. Perhaps some day I will.

Ring-Necked Pheasant

SUMMER

Cardinal. Adult male

Since we feed wild birds throughout the year, we have the pleasure of seeing many of them bring their young to our feeder to give them seed.

One evening, I was watching one of the local cardinal families at the feeder, the young ones calling incessantly, all with drooped wings aflutter, necks craning to be fed. The adult male was very attentive to their seemingly unending appetites and kept trying to fill those bottomless pits.

The Kentucky cardinal, or redbird, is the official state bird of seven states; no other bird can make that claim. The western meadowlark has been chosen by six states and the mockingbird by five.

The color of the male cardinal is a delight at all times of the year; and his voice, which can be tuned to any of a variety of songs (but all definitely cardinal quality) is bold and clear. The female, too, sings quite well, which is not usual in the world of birds.

As is true with many species where the male is brilliantly colored, he takes little part in nest activities, lest his bright color betray the nest and young. He does, however, bring food to the lady of the house as she incubates her eggs. When the young have left the nest, he takes over the entire job of feeding them. Mama, in the meantime, already is sitting on more eggs.

Most often with birds, the male defends the territory where the nest has been built, but the female cardinal shares this task with her mate, and with great vigor will defend the territory they have staked out from others of her sex and breed.

Cardinals are considered permanent residents wherever they are found, but some migration or travel does occur among individuals. This has been learned from banding experiments.

When they have left the nest, all young ones still resemble the female—until they change their feathers for the first time for fall and winter. This is called "postjuvenal molt" and it is with this new set of feathers that the sexes take on their characteristic male and female plumage. This plumage is lighter than the adults', however, because the tips of the feathers are lighter in color. These tips disappear by wearing off, and the bird's color underneath appears brighter and brighter by spring.

When the second fall and winter comes, the young cardinals will have changed feathers completely a second time, but then they will be the full color of an adult bird—even the large bills are much redder.

In Kentucky, the eggs of the cardinal are usually laid by the first week in April, and later another clutch is laid. Often a third family is raised before the season is out.

These handsome birds are much loved in the eastern United States, especially in the South where they are even more numerous than in the North.

Wild Herbs as Medicines

The names ginseng, yellowroot, bloodroot, alumroot, foxglove, mayapple, and ginger are familiar to mountain people of the Appalachians. They are familiar to me, for my father derived a substantial amount of his income in the mountains from collecting these herbs. I have filled a few sacks myself.

Ginseng seems always to have been a premium plant; today it is bringing $18 a pound on

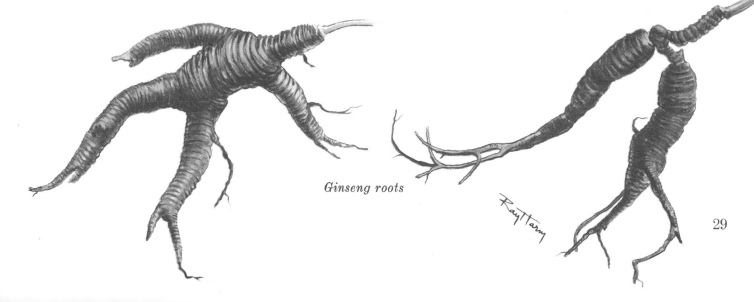

Ginseng roots

29

the American market. "Sang," as the mountaineers call ginseng, has a sweet, licorice-like taste and is used most extensively in China. It is doubtful that the root has any medicinal value other than as a demulcent, but Asians use it both medicinally and as a good-luck charm. Educated Chinese deny this latter use; nevertheless, in the Orient, the price of the root is often set by its shape. The most prized roots are said to be those which resemble the shape of the human figure. (I have sketched such a root and also a more ordinary root taken from a plant dug near my home.)

The plant grows slowly, preferring shady north slopes. It should be dug in the late summer or fall when the root is at its best. Because of its value, ginseng is no longer a common wild plant. It is rare, if not entirely missing, in many areas.

Yellowroot also needs the cool shade of the hilly, open forest. Seeds on the plants turn scarlet red and resemble a large red raspberry. The root of this plant (dug in autumn) is a bright yellow; the Indians are said to have used the juice as a dye. Like many other wild herbs, yellowroot is an active ingredient of modern drugs.

Kentucky, Tennessee, and North Carolina, combined, are the largest source of herbs gathered wild for use in modern botanical drugs in America. Since the advent of synthetics, few people realize the extent to which plants are still used in the manufacture of medicines. The present market for plants used medicinally exceeds $250 million annually and is increasing.

In recent years, many of the so-called "home remedies," pioneer and Indian "cures" of botanical origin, have been found to be scientifically sound, and, in some cases, to contain additional properties, heretofore unknown, for use in modern medicine.

I have used red clover flowers, cherry bark, and honey together effectively for a cough syrup. I have stopped bleeding of a small wound with astringent plants such as cranesbill (alumroot or wild geranium) or the alum-like powder from puffball mushrooms. A slice from bethroot applied to a bee or hornet sting is a soothing poultice.

Many other home remedies, available for just the picking, are not to be laughed at—some of them really work.

·Don't Pick the Wildflowers

Cool mountain hollows are a different world on a hot summer day; they smell fresh and are lush with growth. The clear, running water is a sound and a refreshment not easily walked away from.

Farther down our hollow there are several little waterfalls, and just above one of these grows a single, yellow lady's slipper on the bank near the base of a sugar maple. It's one of my favorite spots.

April into May are the months for the lady's slipper here at home, and this two-foot high wildflower is one of the most handsome of the wild orchids; and it is fragrant, unlike most wild orchids.

30

Yellow lady's slipper

It usually grows individually in shaded, moist soils; only occasionally a clump of two or more may be found. It is a rich, bright yellow and enjoys a comparatively long flowering period.

To me, its size and solitary growth give it a regal air—an "aristocrat" of the wildflowers.

There is a wild orchid that grows in the uplands throughout the winter. In some sections of the country this orchid is called "Adam and Eve." In others it is called "putty-root." It makes its presence known during late summer and the cold months by growing a large, single, tough green leaf up from among the fallen leaves of the forest floor.

By spring, when the flower is in bloom, the leaf is withering away, and the flower is left standing by itself on a single stalk, which may be twenty inches tall.

Another wild orchid, similar to the putty-root, is the crane-fly orchid. It has delicate flowers resembling an insect. It does not get together with its leaf at all! By the time this flower blooms in the summer, its wintergreen leaf with a purple color on the underside has long since withered away.

Neither orchid is a showy type. Each displays a cluster of small, dull, bronze-colored flowers. Nevertheless, close inspection reveals a delicate beauty.

What is an herb? Herbs, unlike trees and shrubs, can generally be defined as plants that do not carry their buds through the winter, but each year die back to the ground. They depend upon their roots or seeds to get them above

31

Bloodroot

ground again each season. This means that the bulk of our wildflowers are herbs.

What is a weed? Well, naturally, weeds are plants that grow where they are not wanted. Some of our most beautiful wildflowers are considered weeds by farmers—and rightly so, I suppose. This makes almost any wildflower that stands in a man's way a weed. Daisies, black-eyed susans, dandelions, sticktights, teasles, thistles—the list is unending—all are weeds, or beautiful wildflowers, depending upon which side of that fence you are on. Most weeds are also herbs.

There are three types of herbs: *annuals* (and there are many of them) live one year and rely only upon their seed for future life of their kind. *Biennials* have roots that live only two years, storing up food made by their leaves the first year and producing seeds in the second year to insure future propagation. The thistle is a biennial. *Perennials* have roots that remain year after year, branching out and sending up new plants each season. An example is Kentucky's state flower, the goldenrod; also the wild morning glory is a perennial. (And is it ever!)

There are fewer biennials than the other two types.

Conservation of wildflowers should be important to us. As our nation progresses and the population increases, we lose more and more wildflowers to land-clearing for spreading suburbs, housing, industry, and highways—and to people who thoughtlessly pick them for pleasure.

Picking wildflowers should be discouraged because the majority of them are annuals; not only does the picked blossom soon die, but the plants and their progeny that would have grown the following year from the picked flower's seeds are lost forever.

There are many seed companies that sell about every kind of wildflower seeds for wildflower gardens. This would be the way to have your own wildflowers to enjoy.

Mother Bird Makes Morsels Bite-Size

While I was watching a nest of indigo buntings from a blind, the parent bird brought a large grasshopper to the nest.

As the young ones stretched their scrawny little necks upward to be fed, she shoved the entire grasshopper into one of the wide-open mouths and deep into its throat. It was much too large a morsel, so the little one just sat there, unable to do anything with that huge grasshopper stretching its small throat and overflowing its mouth.

The parent cocked her head several times, looking the situation over, then reached down and removed the insect. After nipping the grasshopper in half, she crammed the abdomen-half down the little one's throat again; but still it was too much. Finally, the mother bird pulled the grasshopper back out, then began to tenderize it and reduce the size further by kneading it in her bill until the size was equal to the

Indigo buntings

task. I felt relieved when she got the job done properly.

Bird nests are about 20 per cent successful in producing adult birds. If it were not for the special adaptations in the evolution of bird eggs, I'm sure this figure would be even lower.

The very colorful eggs of some birds are left undisturbed by nest-raiding animals because most are repulsive to the taste. Many colorful eggs are protected also by camouflage. The killdeer, for example, lays such eggs on the bare ground; they defy detection from their background, even from a short distance. On the other hand, some ground-nesting birds lay eggs that can be seen easily, but this is compensated for by the adult incubating bird's own effective protective coloration.

Birds that lay their eggs in precarious places, on cliffs and hillsides, have eggs that will not roll away because they are shaped much like a top, small at one end, which limits the egg to rolling in a tight circle.

Birds that are greatly subject to predators, such as ducks, quail, and grouse, must compensate for greater losses; they lay clutches of eggs in greater numbers than the tree-nesting birds. A quail, for instance, lays twelve to eighteen eggs, while a tree nester, such as the cardinal, lays only two to four.

Bird methods of feeding the young vary too, depending upon the species. Some birds develop enough within the egg, that at hatching time they are fairly well able to move about and feed themselves. Ducks, geese, swans, quail, pheasant, and grouse are examples of "precocial" birds. Many of the precocial type are simply led to food by their parent.

Robins, cardinals, sparrows, and the like are helpless when hatched, so they spend a period of time in the nest, cared for by their parents. Such is the case with our young indigo buntings. These are called "altricial" species.

Some species gather food and swallow it, later regurgitating the partly digested food into the mouths of their young; this aids digestion for the young ones. Doves and pigeons feed their nestlings "pigeon milk," which is produced from the walls of the pigeon's crop. The young pelican plunges its head far down to the shoulder level of its parent to get regurgitated fish—quite a sight, believe me!

Wild Animals Not in Distress

Often I get calls or letters from people who have discovered some wild creature's baby "in distress." Assuming that the parent animal has "deserted," or that the young one has wandered away from its den and become lost or has fallen from its nest, the well-meaning individual attempts to help out the youngster. Most often, this is not the right thing to do.

A young fawn is discovered curled up, all alone, and the discoverer just naturally figures that it has been deserted by the doe. Actually, this is a normal part of the fawn's life. Being too small at birth to accompany its mother on her travels for food, the fawn spends the first weeks of its life curled up in one spot, being still and blending in with the background for protec-

Young robin being fed a worm

tion. The doe returns at intervals to give it milk until it has grown enough to follow her about.

Young bird fledglings are the most common victims of apparent distress. There are some mistaken beliefs about how young birds leave their nests. Parent birds do *not* teach their youngsters how to fly before or after they leave the nest—this comes quite naturally—nor do they force the youngsters out of the nest when they think it is time. It is also a mistaken belief that the parent birds withdraw food from the young ones, thus forcing them to leave the nest for food.

Nestlings become fledglings quite on their own. Actually, the parents may continue to feed the young ones for weeks and sometimes months after they leave the nest. I must qualify this paragraph by adding that, of course, it does not apply to all species but is generally the case.

When a young altricial bird leaves its nest, it is at a disadvantage for a few days because its tail is usually still quite short and it is without the strength of maturity. Heavily dependent upon the parent birds for food, the youngster will "cheep" almost incessantly so that the adults can locate its perch or place on the ground to bring it food. This "cheeping" is often mistaken for distress by well-meaning people.

At such a time, especially in or near cities, people who feel concerned may be of more help to the fledgling by keeping a watchful eye on it from a distance, discouraging cats in particular and dogs and children in general from disturbing it. By and large, the parent birds can best care for it, and it doesn't take many hours for

Whitetail doe and fawn

37

the young bird to gain strength and flying ability to take it out of harm's way.

If a nestling falls from a nest or is blown out by a storm or some other accident, it is best to return it to its nest, if possible. Humans can do only second best, and more often do damage that can result in death for a wild animal by feeding it adulterated foods such as bread and chemically treated or heat disturbed liquids such as pasteurized milk. These foods, although eaten by man, produce grave consequences to the highly keyed and sensitive systems of birds or other wild animals.

꧁·Survival Is a Daily Challenge

We heard a commotion outside—the frantic chirping of alarmed robins. We hurried out and found that a crow had settled into the top of a tree in which the robins had built their nest and hatched their young.

The crow ignored us along with the angry harassment of the parent birds as he dropped down limb by limb closer to the nest.

Carmella, distressed, asked if there wasn't something we could do to save the young birds, and I told her I didn't think so because, if that crow didn't raid the nest now, he'd surely come back later. For the moment this answer had as much effect as gasoline on a fire, so I ran for the rifle, knowing that a crow usually is gun-shy.

When I returned, the crow was flying from the nest with the flesh-colored form of the young robin in its grasp. The adult robins were still flying violently at the crow—but to no avail.

Such is the way of nature, whether we like it or not. I learned long ago to let such occurrences in the wild cause me a minimum of discomfort. A fox or a hawk takes a quail; a snake strikes a rabbit; animals kill other animals for food as they have for many centuries before man. Their life demands it.

Various species of wildlife have evolved in different ways that allow for such losses. One way is that the young in large families have more of a chance for some of them to escape predators and live to have large families of their own, since this tendency toward multiple births is hereditary. Those individuals with small families have little chance of surviving. Thus an entire species will have in its nature the genetic factor for large families.

For instance, the quail, like many of its relatives who build nests directly on the ground, is able to resist annihilation by the many ground-roving predators through laying large clutches of eggs, often as many as eighteen. Even if the hen is fortunate enough to hatch her entire clutch of eggs, the chicks still have a long, precarious way to go to reach adulthood.

In contrast, a cardinal, whose nest has more protection in the trees, accordingly gets by with laying fewer eggs, only two to four; but the cardinal has hazards too, like the robins.

Incidentally, after the crow incident, the robins in the beginning of this story abandoned their nest, built another, and tried again; they successfully ended the season with two broods of young.

Parent robins attack nest-robbing crow

Ray Harm

39

Wood duckling

Little Wood Ducks Are "Paratroops"

Early this spring I was attracted by two small ducks flying past my window. I followed their swift flight past the house and watched them fly in close formation as they made a wide reconnaissance around the lake.

Because my house extends out over a bluff some two hundred feet above the lake I could watch the entire course of their exploratory flight. After making several circles, the ducks must have decided it was safe, for they dropped down together, gliding into a familiar, delicate landing some twenty yards offshore.

The next morning I found them still on the lake and making explorations up into the woods during the day. I was gratified that this summer the lake would host a family of "woodies."

Wood ducks are undoubtedly America's most colorful duck. Their breeding range covers practically the entire eastern United States, with very little of it extending beyond our borders. They nest in trees, using hollow branches or cavities in the trunks or vacated woodpecker holes. They are easily attracted to man-made nesting boxes erected around ponds, lakes, or streams, and their ability to gain entrance to the recommended four-inch hole is remarkable.

Their speed while entering the hole is fantastic! Often I have watched a duck fly into a nesting hole, and my eye automatically goes to the opposite side of the tree or box, expecting to see the duck come bursting through. They don't seem to slow down at all when they reach the hole! In the deep woods they dart swiftly and gracefully among the branches of the trees.

One might wonder how the ducklings manage to get to the ground after hatching in one of the very high front doors. The hen simply flies to the ground, calls, and one by one the little ones appear at the entrance like paratroopers and "Geronimo" into the wild blue.

Since they cannot fly at all in their downy plumage, it is really a matter of that first step being a "lulu." Somehow they all survive the fall (which may be over fifty feet), gather themselves up, and follow Mamma on down to the water.

Wood ducks do not have the classic "quacking" voice that one usually associates with ducks. They send out an eerie whistling tone that varies, depending upon the circumstances, from a soft "mewing" by the hen to a broken, loud, flutelike call from the drake.

Being woodland birds, woodies often eat food from the forest such as nuts, berries, and fruits. The grinding power of the gizzard of some birds is extraordinary; the wood duck is one of these, its gizzard crushing and grinding acorns, beechnuts, and hard seeds swallowed whole.

It is difficult to distinguish one species of duck from another in flight at a distance, but one outstanding characteristic of the woodie is its downward-pointed bill while flying. It also has an unusually long tail for a duck. It is not easily confused with others, however, when it is close enough for one to see its striking pattern of color. Even the little female woodie (drab like most female ducks) is far more colorful than the females of our other duck species.

〽·Poison Ivy, Oak, and Sumac

Of the many poisonous plants found in the United States, none is as well known as poison ivy. It is often mistakenly called "poison oak" though actually it does not resemble that plant, nor does it share the same growing range. Another commonly known plant is poison sumac, which is easily separated from other sumacs by its preferred habitat of marshy areas.

Poison ivy, once identified, is easily recognized. The three leaves alone, however, should not be relied upon for positive identification, because there are a great many plants in the woods and fields that produce three leaves. The edge of the leaf of this vine is peculiar in that it is usually uneven. It grows in a number of habitats and sometimes in great abundance.

Poisoning cannot be contracted unless the leaves of the plant have been bruised or broken and the juices or essence of the plant picked up directly or transported in some way by secondary carriers such as pets, shoes, clothing, smoke from burning ivy, or garden tools. It is even possible that infection from poison ivy may be passed along to human beings by insects that have fed from the leaves and then alighted upon bare skin. I have heard and read that one may build up resistance to poison ivy by eating leaves of the plant in increasing amounts. This does not confer immunity, and definitely should *not* be attempted.

Eastern poison oak is a shrub confined primarily to the East and the Gulf Coast of the United States, except that its range does extend

Top: poison ivy; middle: poison sumac; bottom: poison oak

American Butterflies

northward into Arkansas, Oklahoma, and Missouri, and I have seen it in far western Kentucky. Poison oak is not a vine and does not usually share the same habitat with poison ivy because of the different soil requirements.

Poison sumac is found in the East but is confined to wet areas. The fruits hang downward from the stem and are cream colored, features that also distinguish it readily from other sumacs which have erect, red fruits.

The best prevention of poisoning from these plants is the ability to recognize them and keep a safe distance. If you are aware of a susceptibility to the poison, there are medical precautions to take. Your doctor should be consulted before the season (late fall), so that he can prescribe treatment that can prevent infection.

How Earthworms Operate

It is surprising, when we stop to think of it, how little we know about the things around us in our day-to-day living.

The common earthworm, for instance, is looked upon daily by thousands of fishermen who know little more about it than its ability to attract fish. Most people do not realize the earthworm's economic value to man.

The earthworm makes the soil suitable for supporting life by digging deep into the earth —as much as six or eight feet—and bringing the subsoil to the surface. (It swallows the soil, digests the nutritive matter in it, and deposits the rest on top of the ground near its burrow.)

In this "plowing the ground," the little worm aerates the soil and makes passages for necessary surface water to penetrate; it carries leaf matter and other organic material into the ground; its digestive process provides waste material, which serves as fertilizer.

All of this, as any good farmer knows, is good for the soil. The workings of one earthworm, multiplied by the many thousands in a given acre, do much for us. It has been estimated that the earthworms in one acre of ground will turn over some eighteen tons of earth during a five-year period!

Earthworm

Take a closer look at the earthworm. Did you know that it has feet? Well, not really feet as we know them, but they are used for getting about, for the worm does *not* move as a snake does, with overlapping scales on its belly. We find on the underside of each segment of a worm's body (except the first and the last) four pairs of protrusions called "setae" which serve as locomotive appendages. They enable the animal to grasp things and move about.

When the earthworm feeds (which is during the night) it anchors itself to its hole and stretches out on the surface of the ground. Feeding upon almost anything, including earth, it maintains contact with its hole by attachment while outside, so that upon threat of danger it can pull itself back into its hole to safety with amazing speed.

One trick to get worms to come to the surface is to pound a wooden stake into the ground and rub a board or branch across the top of it. The vibration often causes the worms to come up.

During daylight hours, the earthworm remains in the upper part of its tunnel with the bare tip of its "nose" at the surface. This is the part of the worm that the sharp-eyed robin must discover when searching for food. It is an old misconception that when a robin stops and cocks its head to the side it is listening for the body movements of the earthworm. There has been considerable argument about this among bird watchers but I am convinced that the bird is focusing his eye on the worm's location rather than listening to it. (The best focusing from the eye of a robin is done to the side— from one eye—unlike man's binocular vision.)

It isn't knowledge of birds that forms my opinion, however, but the knowledge that the worms usually are not moving about during the day, when the robin feeds.

The youth of an earthworm is determined by the absence of the wide band around the forward part of its body. This band, found on adults, is slipped off the worm during reproduction, and the two sides seal together, forming a cocoon for the growing baby worms inside.

Meadowlarks Go Unnoticed on Ground

One of the most common birds I see in the open areas as I drive through the country is the meadowlark. Its bright-yellow-and-jet-black necklace makes it one of the most brilliantly colored birds to be found in North America.

I suppose that because it spends so much of its time on the ground, and because the tan, dead-grass color of its back is not very striking, it is often overlooked. Sometimes, though, meadowlarks perch on a fence rail or post or even a telephone wire, revealing the brightest lemon-yellow color.

In the West, the meadowlark looks much like its eastern relative, but when it sings, the difference between the eastern and western varieties becomes obvious. The eastern bird has a long, slurring whistle, the western a much more musical song.

From a distance, the flight of meadowlarks is

Meadowlark

45

easy to identify in silhouette, because it is slow, sometimes looking more like a labored flutter than graceful motion. Meadowlarks are easily identified from behind by the broad, white outer tail feathers displayed when the tail is spread in flight.

Occasionally, I come upon the nest of this bird in the fields. It is built on the ground from grasses and is especially interesting because of the roof built to protect the eggs and incubating birds. I recall once intentionally trying to find a meadowlark's nest by watching the adults go to and from it while feeding their young, but it seems characteristic of them not to land or take off near their nest. They often land many feet away and walk in. And, incidentally, they *do* walk, putting one foot ahead of the other—unlike the hopping of sparrows or robins, or most birds for that matter.

In Kentucky, meadowlarks are found to be even more in evidence, because many northern nesting birds winter in the South. Something more to make our winters pleasant. Meadowlarks are, from all points of view, an asset to man. Their diet is harmful insects and weed seeds primarily. Grasshoppers constitute a large percentage of their meals.

Too often, boys take advantage of this ground-loving, slow-flying bird with their BB guns. I recall a man who told me proudly that he could fill a room with the "field larks" he shot as a boy.

It is a federal offense to shoot any songbird, and I encourage reporting to the local game warden anyone found shooting songbirds. Such "sport" is senseless and irresponsible.

From top to bottom: Kallima butterfly, spicebush butterfly larva, moth side view, Io moth, tobacco hornworm

✐·An Insect's Way of Life

Most animals that are without apparent means of defense are provided with protection of one kind or another. This protection, however, is sometimes deceptive in character, and not the teeth, claws, or cunning of more aggressive animals.

Some of these deceptions are remarkable. There is, for example, a large butterfly of India that is so complete in its deception that it is well worth mentioning here. It is called the Kallima. The upper sides of its wings are colorful but, when it alights, it folds its wings together so that only the undersides are exposed. The likeness to a dead leaf hanging from a twig is perfect.

When the tails of the wings touch the branch upon which it rests, they look just like the stem of the "leaf" which appears to carry a midrib through its entire length; such is the pattern of the wing. The veins of the insect's wings even look like the veins of a leaf. As if this were not enough, nature has provided two "holes" in the wing design of this butterfly, to give it even more the appearance of an insect-eaten leaf.

We have many butterflies and moths that have much the same type of protection. Some moths, when they alight on trees, do so in an upside-down position, and the curve of their structure makes them look like twigs of the tree. Some alight sideways, with their wings open, and their particular wing pattern blends in beautifully with the tree they are on.

The Io moth has two very convincing "eyes" to frighten a would-be predator. The green caterpillar of the spicebush swallowtail butterfly has markings that resemble the front end of the common green snake. The tobacco or tomato hornworm, larva of the sphinx moth, has a "horn" sticking up on its tail end and, when threatened, it will raise its tail and wave that horn around as though it could sting—but it is harmless. Nevertheless, it probably discourages many insect-eaters.

Ironically, some animals *need* to be very colorful for their protection. It is no accident that hornets, yellow jackets, velvet ants, and some bees are brightly colored with yellow and black. I'm sure you will agree that this coloration makes it easy to identify them quickly. So what do we do? We leave them alone, of course! Although they have effective stingers, this would not save their lives if they were attacked by an insect-eating animal, but, once stung, the animal does not soon forget this bright color combination. Therefore, these colorful insects are, with some exception, left alone.

Other species of insects which are not of the stinging variety have developed colors that, in a sense, mimic the stinging ones and so, deceptively, ride their coattail of protection.

✐·Some Unusual Insects

The black widow is America's most poisonous spider, and its bite has been known to be fatal, but I think this has been a bit over-emphasized. From my own experience and observation, I judge them not to be so dangerous as is commonly believed. I have been bitten by the black widow and, although it was quite painful, I suffered no other ill effects.

There are three subspecies of black widows in our country, and the poison may be more potent in one group than another. I do know that some people are more susceptible to poisons than others, and a bite that may not be great danger to one might be fatal to another.

It seems that all spiders have venom to some degree, and this usually varies according to the size of the spider. Also, the size of the animal bitten is probably a factor. The poison (and this includes the black widow's) usually does not immediately, if at all, kill the spider's prey, but immobilizes it to facilitate the further "tying down" of the victim with the sticky web. Spiders have the ability to spin different kinds of threads for different purposes.

Generally, spiders fall into two groups: those that move around and hunt their food, and those that spin a web and wait there for insects to be trapped in it. I am fascinated by webs covered with morning dew and recall many fields in early morning where I have seen hundreds of perfectly constructed webs of orb-weaving spiders, reflecting the sun in a million diamonds of sparkle.

Out-of-doors, black widow spiders may be found under loose rocks, around or over which they build a web which is quite wide (as much as three feet) and funnel-shaped near the entrance, with the sheet of web more loosely built on the perimeter.

Black widows are widespread, from New England to South America, and more common in the South. The female, the dangerous gender, has a red "hourglass" mark (although to me it looks more like two triangles pushed together) on her underside. There is often red striping, or an interrupted stripe, lengthwise on the top surface of her abdomen.

The male of this species has much larger legs, the leg joints are colored brownish, and his abdomen is adorned with stripes of red, bordered with white lines running down the side.

Watching a praying mantis turn its head to look in different directions is quite entertaining and strange. Since no other insect can do this, one tends to attribute an intelligence to the mantis beyond that of other insects.

Mantises are valuable predators, destroying many insects harmful to gardens and crops. They also have been known to attack things many times their own size, including small frogs and salamanders, for food.

It is not uncommon for the female mantis to eat the male after mating, and she may do this to more than one suitor.

After a life of only one season, she leaves a mass of froth-covered eggs that dries to a hard paper-like consistency. Next spring, the egg mass will soften, and the next generation will emerge.

Some of those voracious little ones will eat their brothers and sisters and later they will be busy with many destructive insects that are attracted to plant life. Still later, they will find mates and when summer ends so will that generation, as mantises have been doing for who knows how many thousands of years.

What is more important to an artist than his

Female black widow spider

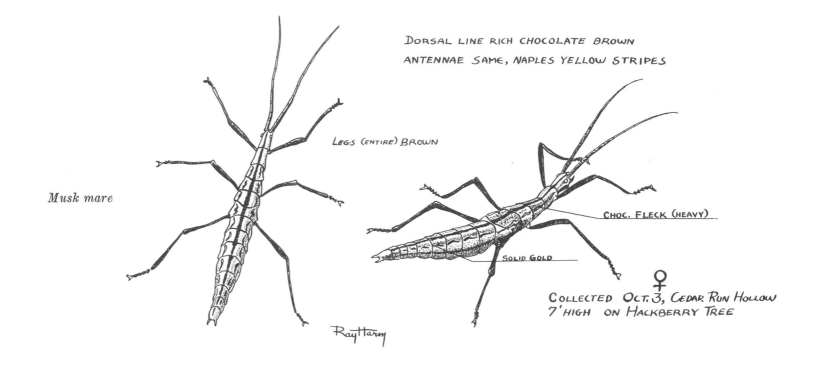

DORSAL LINE RICH CHOCOLATE BROWN

ANTENNAE SAME, NAPLES YELLOW STRIPES

LEGS (ENTIRE) BROWN

Musk mare

CHOC. FLECK (HEAVY)

SOLID GOLD

♀

COLLECTED OCT. 3, CEDAR RUN HOLLOW
7' HIGH ON HACKBERRY TREE

Ray Harm

eyes? I learned a lesson one October when a strange insect I was studying attacked me with a spray that blinded me in one eye. Three days passed before total vision returned.

I was locating persimmon trees on our new property in the Knobs, when I found this odd-looking insect clinging to a hackberry tree, about seven feet up. It was about three inches long, about as wide as a pencil, and resembled another insect called the "walkingstick," except that it was much heavier bodied. It was a beautiful brown color, flecked with bronze or gold on each section of its anatomy. I picked it off the tree and knelt down to look at it when suddenly, from about eight inches away, it sprayed a fog that hit me directly in the right eye.

The pain was excruciating, and I immediately tried to make my eye water as much as possible, to wash out the substance and get some relief. After flushing my eye well at a spring, I took my find home in order to study him further, but this time with more caution! I had come across this same species of insect before, but not with such dire results.

The insect was a musk mare.

Apparently there is much to be done to increase our knowledge about this particular insect. The texts have little information about it other than describing it and classing it in the same family as the walkingstick group. They note also that the musk mare secretes a yellowish fluid when disturbed.

My own experience showed that it is capable of ejecting its fluid in the form of a very effective fog.

You may recall having seen little cone-shaped excavations in the dry dirt or sand back under rock ledges and cliffs (and sometimes under porches and houses) where the ground is seldom exposed to the rain and the dirt is powdery from years of being dry.

Maybe you wondered what made them. At the bottom of those conelike holes there lies buried, head up and patiently waiting, the doodlebug.

The doodlebug in this stage is the larva of an insect that, when it becomes an adult, much resembles a damselfly. The adult is not a strong flyer and is usually out and about at night.

But back to our doodler while he is in the larval stage. He has hatched from an egg and was laid on the bare ground by the adult, and he has dug this funnel-shaped hole to serve as both a home and a trap for his food.

He moves always backward and flips the sand upward with surprising force. The rim of his private crater is approximately an inch to two inches across. An unsuspecting ant or other insect venturing to the rim of this pit is helpless. The loose grains of sand keep giving way under its scrambling feet as it slips and slides down the sloping wall.

If it seems to make any headway at all, our doodlebug, buried at the bottom, causes the walls to shift faster by movements of his head until the exhausted prey inevitably falls right into his two huge, waiting jaws, which also serve as food tubes. He grabs his trapped victim, paralyzes it with a liquid secretion and removes its insides through his tubelike jaws to his own insides.

The doodlebug may be exposed at the bottom of his pit if you gently blow the powdery soil away. Don't blow too hard, lest you blow him out, too, for he is small—only about a half or three-quarters of an inch long.

Female Kingfisher a Beauty

At our home we hear the loud chatter or "rattling" voice of the kingfisher around the lake almost daily. This bird is interesting to watch as it hunts for fish. In fact, its appearance alone is interesting enough.

Kingfishers are not small birds, as birds go, having a wingspread of over twenty inches. They have a large, effective-looking bill and an oversized head topped by a very ragged-looking crest. The oversized head is probably one of the adaptive features in the development of this species, useful in the work of digging their long tunnels into stream banks for nesting, and very likely an aid to their plummeting accuracy as they dive headlong into the water, for they are most successful hunters of fish.

Kingfishers hunt from a perch near or over water; they will often use the same perches

51

Female belted kingfisher

Ray Harm

throughout the season. They also hunt from the air, in flight, where they will hover, helicopter-like, suddenly diving straight into the water, sometimes becoming completely submerged in pursuit of their prey.

Their feet are small, but close inspection will reveal that the middle toe and the outer toe are fused together along the upper joint. I suspect that this, too, is a part of their fitness for use of their feet in removing dirt from the burrows they dig. A burrow may be over ten feet deep into the side of a hill. Quite a tunnel!

Some authorities on birds state that the belted kingfisher's diet varies from water living animals, but I, personally, never have observed this.

In our part of the world the male of most species of birds is more colorful than the female; of course this is protection for the nest, eggs, and young which could be betrayed by a brightly colored mother-bird drawing attention to them. The female birds usually are dull in color, blending into the background for good camouflage.

But the kingfisher is an exception to this; the female of this species is more colorful than the male. She sports a band of robin red across and down the sides of her breast that the male does not have.

And why not? For the nest of the kingfisher is an enlarged hole at the end of a long tunnel in the earth—no need for protective coloration.

So the kingfisher has something in common with present-day humans: the females dress more colorfully than the males.

Skinks' Behavior Fascinating

. In the latter part of June, my son Hap and I were walking along our bottomland when he kicked apart a small, rotten log, exposing thirteen eggs of an off-white color. There, curled alongside, brooding her clutch of eggs, was a female five-lined skink.

Even in the face of her exposure and our presence, she followed her maternal instinct and remained by her eggs—a trait not usually found in most other lizards in America. Ordinarily, lizards simply deposit their eggs in a hole that they dig and then leave, letting nature take care of the rest.

Hap asked if he could take them home to wait until they hatched so that he could watch them emerge from their eggs. I said he could, but he would have to take good care of the female with food while she watched her eggs.

He promised he would, so we carefully gathered up the mother with her thirteen eggs and carried them on to the house, where we put them in a box on our porch. We put some loose forest soil in it along with some leaf matter and decaying wood, gently covering the clutch of eggs.

It was one of the easiest jobs of wild-animal care that Hap ever undertook because early the next morning he came rushing in to tell me, "The skinks are being born!" At that, our entire family went out to see and during the remainder of the day watched all but two of the eggs hatch. The last two emerged sometime before the next morning.

The first one we watched took very little time to appear. First the egg moved and seemed to stretch (the shells of the lizard's eggs are not like that of a chicken, but soft and pliable). A tiny hole appeared and a drop of thick, clear fluid was pushed out by a tiny nose. The nose hesitated for less than a second, the egg stretched again, the hole split and out wiggled a very active skink, stretched out straight for the first time in its life . . . a full two and a half inches.

One of the brightest, iridescent blues imaginable colored the entire tail of this fast-moving little fellow, a coloration which has given the lizard, in some localities, the name "blue-tailed skink." Young skinks lose this blue color of

their tails by the time they are adults.

On the belly of the baby was an enlarged button resembling a chunk of raw meat, all that was left of the food source from which the egg-bound animal drew sustenance. Some of the hatchlings remained in the egg for several hours, with just the tip of the nose protruding. Some lay with the head exposed, finally wriggling free.

We turned them all loose the next morning, and they scampered off in all directions to find something under which to hide. The young ones probably would live several days without eating, still absorbing food from what was left of their large "belly buttons."

The five-lined skink is the most widespread

Female skink and young

skink in the eastern states. The broad-headed skink, another species which is similar but not as common, is much larger. I have seen them more than ten inches long, while the five-lined usually is about six inches in length. The male of both species almost loses his lines at maturity and becomes a brownish color with a rusty-orange coloration either on the chin or head area, depending on the species.

Moth Has Beauty and Strangeness

The other evening, when Hap and I were returning from the lower end of our lake, he spotted a large Luna moth clinging to a sprig growing out of the water near the shore. We headed the canoe over to the spot for a closer look.

The Luna is a beautiful insect. Its pale green wings spread over three inches, with very impressive, long tails on the hind wings. There is a delicate violet color along the leading edge of the front wings. The thick, heavy body is silvery white.

We got to talking about moths, and Hap was surprised when I told him that many moths do not eat at all in the adult stage. Once they have emerged from the cocoon their sole purpose is to lay eggs—and then they die.

Of course, many adult moths do feed, but they cannot chew; like butterflies, they are equipped with a long tube that unrolls and penetrates flowers for sucking nectar. Often,

friends tell me of the "hummingbirds" that visit the flowers of their tobacco plants in the evening. These are really large sphinx moths hovering at the blossoms and drinking nectar in hummingbird fashion.

The effect of light upon moths is interesting. I remember one night last fall when Hap and I were sleeping under a limestone cliff in the woods and our light source was candlelight, he remarked that a moth must be "pretty dumb" to fly right into the flame of the candle (for two or three had done just that).

Moths can't help themselves when they veer toward a light that way. Generally, moths, unlike butterflies, are keyed to low light intensities and consequently are night fliers. There are exceptions, of course, as many are diurnal, or day active.

The moth is neither "hypnotized" nor attracted to a light or flame willingly, but is turned into it automatically as his flight is oriented by it. As the light becomes more intense the closer he gets, he can't help himself from turning right into it. This would not happen if, like butterflies, moths were keyed to a high intensity of light.

Some American moth larvae, or caterpillars, are poisonous to touch; they have venomous, hairlike bristles growing among their other "wooly" hairs. When such a caterpillar is touched, these sharp bristles break, and the venom within is released. This poison can cause simple skin irritation or nausea or even shock in a human, depending upon the person's sensitivity. Fortunately, such poisonous caterpillars are not common.

55

Luna moth

✒·The World of Wasps

Wasps, which include hornets and yellow jackets, to mention only two of many, are closely related to the bees. Many species are social insects, living together in an organized manner. The queens (fertile females), workers (infertile females), and males (called "drones" in a honeybee colony) all help to serve one purpose: propagation and preservation of the species.

Some species are solitary in their habits; that is, the females build nests and care for the young by themselves.

Wasps are smooth-bodied and very narrow-waisted. They are carnivorous, feeding on spiders, caterpillars, and other insects. Bees are hairy-bodied and thick-waisted. They live on pollen, nectar, and the honey they make.

Hornets (and other wasp colonies) do not live through the cold months. Only the young, fertile queens manage to survive by hibernating in small places that afford them shelter.

In the spring the queen wakes and starts building cells for a new nest in which she lays the eggs that will hatch and provide her with a labor force of workers so that she can devote herself to nothing but the laying of eggs for the rest of the summer.

All the eggs will continue to hatch workers until late in the season, when she will lay eggs that hatch into males and females. Some of these young females will be fertilized and survive the coming winter, carrying on as did the queens before them.

Yellow jackets, hornets, and other wasps that build paper nests are an interesting group of insects of considerable concern to man. They can be pretty short-tempered, but under normal circumstances they are not a threat providing they are not unduly disturbed.

It has been said that ounce for ounce, the venom of a wasp or hornet is more toxic than that of a rattlesnake. Although I have read no authoritative source on this, I am not inclined to doubt it; even one little sting can be quite severe. Ironically, I have witnessed many birds actually gulping down one after another stinging insect. Whether they are stung and are immune to the poison, or just not stung, I do not know.

The round, gray, paper-covered nests we see hanging from tree branches are made by hornets. Yellow jackets also build paper nests, but usually dig and enlarge excavations underground as the nests are constructed there. Yellow jackets probably make a poorer grade of paper because the nests are not exposed to the rigors of wind and rain.

Wasp paper is probably the first form of paper known to man. The insects make it by scraping the surface areas of dead wood or other dead plants, chewing it to a pulp, mixing it with their saliva, and spreading it out thinly to dry in the form of paper.

The familiar paper wasp that we see so often under the eaves of roofs does not usually cover its layers of cells with paper.

There is also the mud-dauber, a wasp which builds its nest with balls of mud on rocks or the wood of buildings, often inside buildings.

Honeybees keep perennial colonies and live through the winter. Clustering together during low temperatures, wild honeybees can keep the hive warm enough to protect the queen. They can also use their wings to cool the hive in the summer—sort of "built-in fans," one might say. Honey they make is eaten during the lean months.

Bumblebees and honeybees make their nests of wax. The bumblebees, like the yellow jackets, construct their nests underground, and only the queen lives through the winter.

I'm sure most of you have noticed insect galls, in one form or another, in the woods and fields. Probably the most common ones are

Left: bumblebee; right: yellow jacket

Top: oak-apple gall on red oak (vacated); left: blackberry knot gall (vacated); right: hedgehog gall on chinkapin oak leaf (in use); bottom: goldenrod gall (in use)

Ray Harm

found on oaks, willows, goldenrod, and black-berry plants, but there are many varieties of these sometimes grotesque-looking growths, for many different plants are hosts to the gall insects.

Gall insects deposit their eggs upon the particular plant they have chosen. They are quite selective about this. In many instances they embed the egg in the tissues of a twig, stem root, flower, fruit, or leaf.

The adult gall wasp lays its eggs upon the veins of oak leaves. Later, as each egg hatches, the larva eats its way into the vein; the cellular growth of the plant increases, and the vein around the tiny "worm" begins to swell rapidly, forming a golf-ball-sized house which also provides food for the insect.

The larva, having eaten until fully grown, pupates (enters the intermediate stage between larva and adult insect). One more transition and it emerges through the outer skin of the oak apple a full-fledged adult wasp about a quarter of an inch long, complete with four wings.

This completes the cycle. The new adult's immediate job is to start the cycle all over again by mating, then producing more eggs on other oak leaves.

Herons and Egrets from the Deep South

Whenever we come from the woods into a clearing such as our lake, it is with deliberate slowness and concealment, so that we may enjoy seeing whatever wildlife strangers the lake may have attracted.

One day in August, Hap and I emerged quietly from the woods at the edge of our lake to find a pleasant surprise. The usual ducks and kingfishers were sharing the lake with two glistening, snow-white birds. I immediately recognized these long-necked visitors as immature little blue herons because I could see on the closer one the powder-blue bill with black tip, a field mark I learned well in the swamps of the Deep South where I had made many sketches of them.

The nearer (call it the first) bird was swallowing one of the new bass I had recently stocked the lake with, and so occupied, it did not see us. The second bird, farther away, did see us and rose from the shallow water in picturesque flight. The first bird was quick to follow.

As they wheeled around to head down the shore line of the lake I got a closer look at the second bird and saw that it was not a little blue heron but a snowy egret, a cousin of the little blue. With their undersides exposed as they turned, I could see the bright yellow feet at the end of the shiny black legs of the second bird, a showy color contrast and definite field mark.

These herons are not small birds; they have a wingspread of better than three feet and are very graceful in flight. They alighted in the very tops of the high trees overlooking the lake, and it looked as though they would never be able to hang on as the small branch tips swayed up and down under their weight. Stop swaying they did, though, appearing quite out of place

Above: snowy egret;
below: little blue heron

in the unswamplike setting of the Kentucky knobland.

Neither of these birds is very rare, but in Kentucky, as in much of the rest of the East and places farther north, they are found only as occasional wanderers from the deeper South which is their main breeding region.

The little blue heron is very white until it matures. With adulthood, it attains its gray-blue color. And even though not a small bird, it is a small heron compared to the great blue heron. Therefore, the little blue heron is what its name implies.

The snowy egret is of special interest to me because, like its cousin the common egret (a larger bird), it was on the brink of extinction years ago. Commercial plume hunters killed egrets on the nest, plucking their long beautiful breeding plumes from their backs to sell for use as decorations for ladies' hats. Thanks to in-the-nick-of-time legislative action, I can now show my son one of these impressive birds on our own land.

·Our "Rain Crow" Is a Cuckoo

Summer is the season for the "rain crow." Many an old-time farmer—and many a modern one, too—will tell you rain is coming when the rain crow calls frequently. Why the name "crow" would ever be attached to this bird is beyond me, for, as my picture indicates, there is no similarity between the two birds.

Properly called yellow-billed cuckoos, these

Yellow-billed cuckoo

birds are magnificent in my book, and certainly very graceful; their movements in the trees are without flaw as they slip from branch to branch in search of insects. This bird is almost entirely insect-eating and is especially noted for the great number of tent caterpillars and fall webworms it consumes. Caterpillars constitute nearly 50 per cent of its diet and, as far as I know, no caterpillar is safe from this bird, including the spiny larvae of the Io moth, which are poisonous even to human touch.

The beauty and grace of the rain crow is no indication of its ability to build a neat nest. Its nest is even more flimsy than that of a mourning dove. How it holds both the eggs and the bird is perplexing, for it is hardly more than a crude platform of a few sticks. Sometimes the bird will lose eggs to the wind when away from the nest. At this writing there are young ones not five hundred feet from our house, and their nest is so sparse that the two nestlings and one yet unhatched egg can be seen through it from ten feet below.

Rain crows are shy birds, more often heard than seen. Frequently, people ask me to identify the voice they hear so often without being able to locate the source. They are often surprised to learn that it was a bird calling, thinking the source to be from some mammal. The call is quite loud and carries well, but it is difficult to describe. I should characterize it as "clucking," and unmusical at that!

Because it is almost entirely insectivorous, the rain crow is very much a migratory bird and spends the winters in South America. Its migratory flight is made at night.

The European relatives of the cuckoo are well known as parasites of other species of birds; they lay eggs in other birds' nests, leaving the incubating of the eggs and care of the young to foster parents. It is on record that our American cuckoos have occasionally reverted to this practice.

Primarily a bird of the forest, cuckoos may also be seen in city parks and around homes. They certainly should be encouraged, for their food habits make them a valuable asset to man; they destroy many harmful insect pests without any disturbance to other forms of life.

Animals That Are Fun to Watch

One of the most entertaining animals to watch is the chipmunk. There is no end to their antics with each other in competition for the corn. Often I have counted as many as six of them on the ground and in the tree waiting nervously to fill their pouches at our corn skewers. (The one on the corn usually will not permit a second one there with him.)

The capacity of their cheeks is fantastic. Full pouches of seed can make the front end of this tiny animal three times its normal size. This pouch saves many trips to their burrows where they store the food for winter or for the extremely hot months in summer, which time they spend deep in their cool earthen burrows.

In the East, these small animals (six inches, excluding tail) often are called ground squirrels, but people in the West differentiate between a ground squirrel and a chipmunk. They are different animals, although related, being members of the rodent family.

The chipmunk's diet is varied, includes many berries, acorns, and other nuts. He will sometimes take grain (but surely not enough to be a real concern to man) and will eat insects, snails, salamanders, and worms. His diet will sometimes include cultivated flower bulbs (much to the dislike of the flower gardener), but people who live in chipmunk areas combat this by planting their bulbs in wire baskets slightly larger than the bulb. Mice, moles, and rabbits are more difficult to control.

We had been clearing out some trees when suddenly, from out of nowhere, a mother squirrel landed with a "swish" on my pantleg, whisked downward, then scurried back and forth along the felled tree, searching for her broken nest.

I sat down on the hornbeam to watch the mother's activity. She was about nine inches long, tail and all; and slate gray in color except for her little white belly.

She quickly found the nest with her four young ones in it. She rolled one of them over and over in her front paws to get a good hold on it. Then, taking her baby in her mouth, she scampered down the length of the fallen tree to the ground over to the edge of the clearing, and up a standing dead beech to an abandoned woodpecker hole about forty feet up, near the top.

This procedure was repeated until all four young ones were tucked securely into their new home.

These eastern flying squirrels, which are common in our area, are nocturnal, sleeping during daylight hours. This, of course, is the main reason we see very little of them.

In comparison with other squirrels, they are much smaller, an adult weighing only three to four ounces. The flying squirrel usually builds its nest in vacant woodpecker holes, with bedding of wild grapevine, mosses, dried grasses, leaves, etc. Its food includes wild grapes, berries, nuts, a variety of seeds, many insects, and other foods, depending upon what the current season yields.

Of course the flying squirrel does not really fly at all. It simply glides with the greatest of ease atop its own parachute formed by an extra skin between its fore and hind legs. The glide may cover surprising distances, but always it is from a higher to a lower spot.

This year, Hap saw his first black squirrel.

With great exuberance he told me all about this rarity—the conditions, the tree, what the squirrel did, how coal-black it looked, and then he looked at me as though he expected me to express some doubt that he really had seen such an animal.

But I didn't. I told him he had seen his first black gray squirrel. He was quick to insist, "No, it was all black—black as tar!"

I explained that, infrequently, a gray squirrel will have a litter containing one that is pure black. This is called a "melanistic color phase."

Melanism means there is an abnormal development of pigmentation of the skin, hair, or feathers of an animal. This is the opposite of albinism, which is a lack of pigment in the skin, eyes, and hair; the hair may be pure white.

64

Eastern chipmunk

Ray Harm

65

Gray squirrel (black phase)

66

Albino gray squirrels also show up occasionally. Olney, Illinois, has gained considerable fame from the strong bloodline of albinism found in its gray squirrels. People come from far away to see the several hundred white squirrels in the area, and the community is right proud of them, protecting them by law.

The reason for such a strong line of albinism in these squirrels is a mystery. Usually, this lack of pigment in the skin dies out after several generations in the wild.

✍·Happiness Is Lying Belly to the Sun

The pure joy of being alive was being experienced the other day by a muskrat I observed upon a rock in the middle of our creek. It was a sunny morning and, listening to the constant ripple of the creek upstream mixed in with other woodland sounds, I wasn't unhappy about anything either.

I first spotted him when I noticed him move. I brought him close with my binoculars and dis-

Muskrat

covered he was really living it up! He was upside down, in the ridiculous position a dog sometimes will assume on his back while asleep or getting his belly scratched.

Occasionally he twisted himself back and forth, scratching his back on the rock, stretched his chin out to the maximum and then lay still again—belly to the warm sun.

Once, paddling up to the shallow end of our lake, I was made aware of a young animal by a splash to my side. There swam a young muskrat toward shore; evidently my approach had forced him from a snag jutting up out of the water. If the adult was around, I did not see her. This was a fully-weaned muskrat about the size of an extra-fat, grown chipmunk.

The little fellow swam to shore and began climbing the bank but stopped, motionless, a foot or so out of the water, alongside a rock.

Slowly, I eased the canoe over to the spot, then I reached out and gently picked him up. He seemed very tame, with no inclination to bite (they have very sharp teeth!).

Soon I was climbing the hill to the house with the young one, to show him to the rest of the family. Close inspection revealed the extraordinarily soft fur of the muskrat, especially of young ones. We noted in detail the characteristic vertically flat, silky tail they use to aid their swimming and the partially webbed large hind feet which, covered with fine hair, also take on a silky appearance. Around his sides he was already getting the reddish-colored hair so characteristic of the adult summer color.

Later I took him back and released him in the very spot where he had entered the water when I first saw him.

In large marsh areas I have seen the muskrat's nesting lodges built of various vegetation and mud, beaver-like and dome-shaped. In the knobs where I live, however, I don't look for such structures. Here the dens are at the end of long burrows that begin under the water in the bank and go well back into the ground.

Sometimes muskrats will damage earthen dams with their burrowing, but they also serve many useful purposes both to man and to other forms of wildlife. They are helpful in checking the excessive spread of common cattail, using the roots and lower stalks for food and incorporating the remainder of the plant into their nests and lodge building.

Muskrats are prolific, and the female may be heavy with young again by the time her first litter is weaned after four weeks. They serve also as food for many forms of wildlife.

Woodchucks, Possums, and Skunks

I was climbing the hill, coming up from my spring late one afternoon, when it happened. Just as my head rose above a small ledge of rock I was blasted by an ear-shattering whistle from this large groundhog. He was not two feet from my face!

After the initial shock several echoes seemed to be resounding in my head, but I realized that it was other woodchucks in the hollow repeating the alarm. Anyone who has not heard the loud, shrill whistle of a groundhog has a real experience ahead of him. It is easy to see why he is sometimes called the "whistle-pig."

Woodchucks will climb trees to find an appropriate fork for a lookout spot in which to perch and, more often than not, wherever a woodchuck burrow is found will be a spot that affords a good observation post.

They hibernate very well underground throughout the winter and if, by chance, one is dug up in the middle of that period, he will be found rolled up in a tight ball, not to be awakened.

Living upon tremendous amounts of fat put on in late summer and fall, they will hibernate six months in some latitudes, emerging in the spring much thinner and primarily interested in finding a mate. Their burrows are dug to varying depths, usually recognized by the mound of earth beside it, which the other escape holes do not have.

Often, the "chuck" will have more than one burrow, many feet apart, so that during their feeding excursions one may be closer than another for escape purposes. Burrows of woodchucks, especially vacant ones, are frequently taken over or enlarged by a fox, a skunk, possum, or some other ground dweller.

The best time to observe this animal is in the early morning hours or in the late afternoon when he is out feeding on vegetation such as leaves, tree bark, and berries.

Woodchuck

Female opossum with young

The opossum is the only North American animal with a pouch for carrying its young ones. The tiny, blind newborns (each weighs only 0.16 grams), after being licked clean by the mother, must make a trip "cross country," so to speak, to the pouch—which is about three inches of travel across the mother's fuzzy coat. Each must then locate a nipple inside the pouch, where it attaches itself very tightly.

Many start this trip in the wrong direction and never make it. It's a wonder that any of them complete the trip at all, because the mother does not assist them. About two months of pouch life pass before the young ones start making trips outside.

This animal is a night prowler, as are most of our mammals, and its ability to "play dead" has been studied with much interest by scientists. My own experiences have led me to discover that some possums will not feign death when threatened, doing no more than crouching, with mouth wide open, in a hostile stance. Those that do "play possum" are very convincing, rolling over, tongue hanging out, eyes closed, with every appearance of a dead animal.

It is now believed that the possum does not deliberately exhibit this trait—rather that he falls into a paralytic reaction or stupor when touched. The belief is that an actual stiffening of the joints occurs, due to a paralyzing substance in the body that is activated by nerve impulses. These substances affect the muscles as long as the nerves are reacting from the touch stimulation.

This summer, a friend and I were on horse-back, riding the ridge to a knob above Overalls Fork in the Bernheim Forest. We came upon a little animal that gave us a few minutes of surprise and pleasure. It was a spotted skunk.

We rode up on the little fellow as he was crossing our trail, and in fun I reined over and got in front of him. This pressed him, of course, and he backed off from us, stopping every few steps to threaten us by stamping his little front feet on the ground and then doing a perfect handstand!

He arched his back so much that his "business" end—where his scent glands are located—could be plainly seen from the front, over his spread tail, pointed directly at us. Needless to say, we respected this and didn't press him too closely.

He did this a number of times but when we didn't press him at all, he tried to get around us in order to carry out his intention of getting down into the hollow. Riding away, we last saw him headed that way.

Skunks do not usually give ground when pressed too tightly. They have effective defense equipment and put a lot of confidence in it, but will usually give fair warning before destroying your dignity. I might say right here that "spray" is not a proper word to use in describing a skunk's defense (or should I say offense?). Jetstream is a better term, and I have learned this through personal experience! Ten to fifteen feet is not too great a distance either, and they have a great deal of accuracy. In the skunk's behalf, however, I must say he will seldom "shoot," even in close quarters, if no threatening advance or movement is made.

Insects make up much more than half the diet of skunks. The animals live in abandoned burrows, natural openings in logs, cliffs, and banks; they also dig their own burrows. They are valuable to man in that on their nocturnal excursions they consume enormous amounts of crop-destroying insects. This good far outweighs the damage they may sometimes do to chicks or eggs on a farm.

What Decides Birds' Diet?

Some animals are exceptionally selective in their diets, and, in one case at least, the inability to adapt to a different food (coupled with the draining of fresh-water marsh areas by man) probably will cause the extinction of one handsome species of hawk in our country. This bird, the everglade kite, by virtue of a specially curved bill, is able to extract a particular fresh-water snail from its shell. The snail is now found only in a few restricted, undrained areas and, accordingly, so is the hawk. The everglade kite is now one of our rarest American birds, with as few as fifty individuals left in the country.

Most birds are not so selective, of course, and eat a variety of available foods. Much of what birds eat depends upon their physical and habit adaptations, such as bill length, whether or not they feed during daylight or night, or how specialized they are in flight, strength, sight, etc.

Spotted skunk

72

Bluejays can digest acorns.

73

Starling

74

Bobcat

Generally, only a few species (the more advanced birds) feed upon plant life. In the main, most of them depend upon animal life for food. In the stages of evolution, those birds that enjoy the highest perch on the ladder of development are typified by the "lowly" sparrow. The sparrow's ability to survive upon seeds, and to adapt itself to year-round rugged climatic conditions, is testimony to this high form of development.

There are interesting adaptations that have developed in the digestion of food by birds. Some are downright unbelievable. A bird's stomach is a very specialized piece of anatomy which must compensate for the animal's lack of ability to chew.

Sand and small pebbles are ingested with seeds by sparrows and other seed-eating birds. The gizzard, with its tremendous muscular kneading action, uses this grit to grind up the seed to aid digestion. The intense power of this stomach, in some ducks and other birds, in crushing various nuts is amazing. A turkey's gizzard can crush a hickory nut to bits, and tests show that up to 330 pounds of pressure are required to break some of these nuts. Even the little wood duck swallows whole hickory and pecan nuts; the bluejay swallows large chunks of acorns; all are crushed by the powerful gizzards of these birds.

Birds digest food very quickly. A shrike will digest an entire mouse in three hours; some birds will digest berries in less than twenty minutes. Birds of prey sometimes swallow their food whole, and their stomachs, by glandular action, chemically dissolve all but the fur and bones, which are later regurgitated in a compact ball called a "pellet." I have picked up these dried pellets from the forest floor and broken them open to learn what the bird's eating habits are, simply by identifying the fur and bones found in them.

Tiniest Animals—Loudest Sounds

The other morning I sketched a dove while he was calling—which brought to mind some thoughts I'd like to share with you, along with this drawing, about sounds in nature.

Some of the smallest animals have the loudest voices. The cricket frog (which isn't much larger than a cricket) is very loud, and the powerful voice of the ovenbird fills the woods and belies his modest, six-inch size. Few people know that the ruby-throated hummingbird has a very loud, chattering voice.

Sounds made by animals are not restricted to the voice. Many birds make unusual sounds with special feathers on their tails or wings. Woodcocks have at the end of each wing three narrow, scimitar-like feathers that produce a strange sound while the bird is flying. The loud whistle made by the wings of the ruffed grouse and the bill-clacking of the owl when disturbed are but a few common sounds not made by voice.

Some sounds are increased by saclike resonators that the animal inflates. The swollen throats of frogs and toads while singing are

Mourning dove inflates entire neck skin while calling.

76

good examples; such "bubbles" of skin can cause sound to carry for miles.

The prairie chicken I have observed in the West inflates a sac of bare skin on each side of the neck (as on the frog), augmenting his voice remarkably. The common mourning dove inflates his entire neck skin!

The "mute" swan is not really mute, but there are some animals that do not have the ability to make vocal sounds, such as the pelican or the man-o'-war bird. The common turkey vulture cannot come up with more than awkward "grunting" attempts to vocalize.

Sound-making among animals serves many purposes in the wild, and different sounds can be recognized by the experienced woodsman, enabling him to sit down in the woods and actually follow many of the daily activities of the wild, simply by listening. Some sounds, however, are so high-pitched that the human ear cannot detect them.

There are sounds of calling, gathering, warning, alarm, fright, locating, approach, mating, and even content. There are territorial songs and cries of pain.

A story of life and death is revealed when a rabbit shrieks its distress cry. All is not serene when any one of the many alarm signals is given by birds, or a beaver slaps the water, or a deer snorts, or a woodchuck whistles. Certain notes of the bobwhite are an indication that the covey of them is regrouping after having scattered.

Sometimes a sound will indicate the sex of the species as well as the reason it is calling. Crickets, katydids, and grasshoppers sing incessantly—each with a purpose. Woodchucks chuck, and chipmunks chip (the chipmunk's "chips" are often mistaken for a cardinal's note) and seem to broadcast to others of their kind.

It's Easy to Spot a Goldfinch—from Its Flight

One day, while visiting friends, we were all captivated by the antics of a bright-yellow little bird in the front yard. The brilliant yellow of the bird's body was in sharp contrast to the black wings, tail, and crown atop his head.

He would fly to the tops of the long stems of dandelion seedpuffs, his weight bending the seed heads to the ground where he would eat his fill from them.

Our hostess remarked how much they enjoyed these "wild canaries" in the summer.

I asked, "Why not in the winter?"

She replied, "Well, they fly south in the winter. We never see them here during that time."

I have often heard similar comments about our eastern goldfinch. In the wintertime, this little finch is still around, but it has changed its bright yellow plumage to resemble the more drab olive colors of its mate.

Because the goldfinch is a finch, it has the ability to survive on a variety of seeds, and therefore is perfectly capable of putting up with Kentucky winters. Some goldfinches winter

as far north as the Canadian border.

In the early days, when much less was known about birds, the seasonal color change of plumage on the males of some species led to mistaken "discoveries" of "new classifications." Even Audubon is known to have painted the same kind of birds collected in different seasons, thinking them to be different species.

One outstanding characteristic of the goldfinch is its undulating, roller coaster flight. I have seen them repeatedly rise and drop as much as fifteen feet on their course in flight, often singing their twittering song all the while. This makes it a cinch to identify them in flight, regardless of their small, five-inch size.

Some woodpeckers have a similar flight, but not nearly to the same extent, and besides, woodpeckers are usually found in the woods, whereas we see goldfinches in the fields, benches, and bottoms.

Unlike most birds, goldfinches do not nest until quite late in the summer (July-August) when other species have already started into a second or even third family. There is a record of one nest being discovered with young in it as late as October.

It is well known by ornithologists that the nest this bird builds is ofttimes too well built for its own good. The young have sometimes drowned during a hard rain because the open nest is so tightly constructed it holds water. Goldfinches, on the average, take nine days to build a nest. When the young are born some eleven to fourteen days later, they are fed partly digested seeds regurgitated from the crop of the adult bird.

American woodcock

The goldfinch is the state bird of at least three states, and there is no doubt that the little fellow is deserving of recognition for he is dramatic and colorful. Watch for these birds with the roller coaster flight both summer *and* winter!

The Woodcock Looks Around

Once, in the woods, I came upon an American woodcock. My presence startled it to flight and in trying to escape it flew smack into a tree. Falling to the ground, it quickly recovered and flew again into the woods, this time making good its escape.

I wasn't really surprised to see that happen, as I was aware of the peculiar set of the woodcock's eyes. It can see better where it's been than where it's going.

This bird's eyes are set far to the rear on the side of its head. The bird has a very long, grooved, flexible-at-the-tip bill, which adds to its strange appearance.

The eyes, however, are the main point of interest. Because the bird probes its long bill into the soft earth, searching for insects and worms, the setting of its eyes gives it perfect rear binocular vision while its bill is sunk deep into the ground.

Each eye is capable of seeing more than 180 degrees and, where the vision of one eye overlaps that of the other in the front and back, it has binocular vision. It is thus able to see in a

Ray Harm

79

complete circle without turning its head.

Most birds see best with monocular vision, or from the side of the head. This is true also of some mammals—rabbits and squirrels, for example. As in the woodcock, some mammals also have complete radial vision.

The woodcock reportedly is able to pick up its young and carry it between its legs and body in time of danger. I recall one time when a bird-watching friend and I came upon an adult woodcock which obviously had an injured wing. Somehow it managed to flutter up to a low branch of a nearby apple tree. At the spot on the ground from which it flew crouched a very young, striped, downy chick, too young to fly.

We ran for a camera but when we returned neither the young nor the adult were to be found. We certainly were fooled by the injured wing act! It has not yet been my good fortune to witness the actual carrying of a young one by an adult.

Just this summer, at the bottom of "Coon Den Hollow" on my place, I spooked up three woodcock from under some cedar brush. One flew a short distance from me to alight at the feet of my wife (she could have touched it with her arm outstretched).

I can only attribute this mistake on the part of the woodcock to its looking at me from behind instead of watching for my wife in front.

Considering the crash into the tree and the alighting of the bird near my wife, I'm not really sure that this form of specialization is entirely favorable to the woodcock—although in the long run the advantages seem to outweigh the disadvantages.

Red Bats Are Loners

This summer, my son Hap and I were out looking for oak apple galls to use as models for sketches. We were high on a knob among the oaks and pines where many branches of the oaks are low, within easy reach from the ground. It was a good place to find galls.

At one point in our search, a practiced second look at what first appeared to be a withered leaf revealed a furry ball, a common red bat, hanging in sleep among the oak leaves.

This tree-living mammal is one of our most common (and handsome) bats. The one we found was a female, recognizable by her light orange-buff color, frosted all over with white-tipped hairs. The color of the male is more intense. Both sexes have a contrasting white patch on the neck at the base of the wing, making them quite colorful indeed.

Bats are of two types: cave bats and tree bats. Cave bats are gregarious and, I guess one might say, "hang around together." The tree bats are more colorful than those of the caves; they are also more difficult to study because of their solitary nature. Students of mammals are interested in learning more about such things as their seasonal behavior, migratory paths, and eating-and-roosting habits.

Many have heard the old story that if a bat entangles itself in a woman's hair it presages her death within the year. This of course, is pure superstition. A bat getting into a person's hair is only remotely and accidentally possible.

Bats are nocturnal and in our country are, for the most part, insect eaters. Occasionally

Red bat among oak leaves

one will thump into my studio window at night while catching insects that are attracted to the light. I suspect that the light is responsible for this type of accident when the bat may turn to hunting by eyesight rather than hearing.

It is now well known that a bat hunts by a sort of radar detection called ''echo-location''; its voice sends out ultrasonic sounds while flying. When the sounds bounce back from an object ahead, the bat picks them up by ear and is able to determine the distance by the length of time taken for the sound to return.

Back on the knob, Hap and I gently cut the branch above our sleeping red bat and carried her, still hanging with the oak leaves, back to our home where we caged her awhile so we could study her. Such voracious insect-eaters as bats are beneficial to man, so we were happy to watch her silently fly off that evening—there are plenty of insects around, and she can help keep their number down.

✍·Snakes Arouse Interest—and Tall Tales

When I was a boy in West Virginia, my Uncle Oscar told me the story about the snake that followed him down the road. He had left his mule and was walking to the house for lunch when he noticed the snake was gaining speed on him. Uncle Oscar picked up a little speed himself, and, to his surprise, when he turned to look back, the snake had reached around and grabbed its own tail in its mouth, pulled itself into a wobbly loop, and was rolling like a hoop after him.

As he neared the house, Uncle Oscar could see that he was going to lose the race so at the last moment he made a quick dodge behind an apple tree in the orchard near the house. Just in time, too, for the snake had released the hold on its tail and sailed through the air, lodging itself tail first, like a spear, into the apple tree.

Much shaken, Uncle Oscar ran into the house for his shotgun, calling Aunt Madge to come see the hoop snake in the tree. Returning with the gun, they found the snake had worked itself loose and was gone, but the poison from the snake's tail was so potent that all the apples had fallen from the tree!

This is an impressive story for a young fella to hear, and it stuck with me for a long time. I suspect that after many tellings, Uncle Oscar himself believed it. Since then I have heard various versions and parts of the same story, along with countless other ''snake stories.''

I have a true snake story which gives the blacksnake credit for more brains than I usually attribute to reptiles.

One day my wife Carmella called me into the living room and pointed to a long (over six feet) black rat snake on the floor at our front screen door. The snake was inside the house and its head was raised, cobra-like, so that it could see out through the screen, since the bottom wood section of the door was two feet high. It was slowly moving its head back and forth across the door as if it wanted outside.

As I moved forward to open the door, the blacksnake turned immediately and went into our guest closet nearby. When I followed to catch it, I discovered it had gone under the sill log of the outside wall and down into the hollow cores of the concrete-block foundation where it was safe from me. I left the screen door partly open with a small piece of wood, then we hid around the corner and waited. After some time it sneaked out and off it went into the woods.

This much was at least partly understandable, but a few days later we were flabbergasted to have our attention again brought to the screen door by a black snake's head moving back and forth, just as before, but this time from *outside* the screen door. It was difficult to believe this was the same snake and that it wanted to get back in. Purely out of curiosity, I again propped open the screen door with the block of wood and sure enough, after a short wait, in it came, going directly to the guest closet and into the concrete blocks.

This continued on and off during the summer with some regularity, and almost any time I could check with my flashlight to find the snake coiled up in the foundation wall. We assumed that the snake simply went out to the woods to feed and spent his long in-between times in the cool of the concrete blocks.

The rattlesnake and the copperhead arouse great interest. I suppose their danger to man has caused them to be regarded with trepidation wherever they are found (and made them the subject of many tall tales).

In Kentucky, four of the North American pit vipers are found: the timber rattlesnake, the

Water snake swallowing bullfrog

canebrake rattlesnake (far west Kentucky), the copperhead, and the cottonmouth water moccasin (also west Kentucky).

I should like to point out that snakes do not make unprovoked attacks upon human beings. I have yet to come upon a nonpoisonous snake (with the exception of the hog-nosed snake which pretends to be poisonous) that did not head in the opposite direction. There would have to be some extenuating circumstance to cause any other reaction on the part of the snake.

It is to our advantage, however, to know that our poisonous snakes do not usually react in the same manner. When they are seen, which is very rarely, they are usually much slower-moving (except the cottonmouth in water), than nonpoisonous snakes. But they will, when given the chance, leave the scene.

Black rat snake

If pressed by the threat of danger, they usually coil to give themselves the best position for striking. And, incidentally, the rattler does not always rattle when alarmed. Escape or striking are the defenses of the poisonous snake. Speedy escape is the defense of the nonpoisonous ones.

I have found that copperheads outnumber rattlesnakes hereabouts, and fortunately the copperhead is by far the least aggressive of the four poisonous snakes of Kentucky. I have accidentally stepped within two or three inches of a copperhead and have not been bitten.

Snakes cannot normally strike much more than half the length of their body, and are restricted to much less in water. Snakes *can* strike underwater, and the newborn of all four of these poisonous snakes are capable of injecting venom with a bite. The young copperheads and cottonmouths have bright yellow tails, a good point to remember. Contrary to the belief of some naturalists, these snakes can choose to inject venom or not while biting.

The fangs of a rattler are curved down and backward. They fold up to the roof of the mouth when not in use and there are several spare fangs growing behind the front ones, in case of breakage or loss.

Each side of the lower jaw of all snakes moves independently of the other so that they can alternately twist and pull the prey inward. Each larger upper fang also can be independently thrust forward to get a greater hold upon the prey for swallowing.

You may generally discount reports of seven- and eight-foot rattlers hereabouts. The official all-time record of a timber rattlesnake is seventy-four inches, the average being thirty-six to fifty-four inches. The average copperhead is twenty-four to thirty-six inches long. The largest species of poisonous snake in this country is the eastern diamond-back rattler (record ninety-six inches), a Deep South and Atlantic Coast reptile.

Once, Carmella and I saw something that took us a few minutes to figure out. At first, it looked like the head of a turtle cutting across the water's surface—a turtle with two huge horns on its head! Closer inspection, however, revealed it to be a large, common water snake that had captured a bullfrog and was in the process of swallowing it when we happened by. The snake had swallowed the frog, head first, down to the frog's waist, and its two legs protruded out and up from the corners of the reptile's mouth, looking for all the world like two horns on the snake's head.

Water snakes are often mistaken for the poisonous copperhead snake or for the cottonmouth water moccasin in the South. (In Kentucky, the cottonmouth is found only in the farthest west part of the state.) Poisonous snakes move much more slowly, and copperheads, while not usually found near water, will swim upon the surface; but the water snake dives readily beneath the surface, capable of remaining on the bottom for a considerable length of time.

Unfortunately, sportsmen frequently kill the harmless water snake, thinking mistakenly that it reduces the supply of game fish. Actually, this is contrary to what scientific research has disclosed. Water snakes *improve* game fish

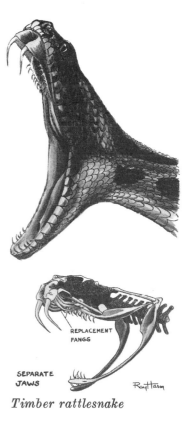

REPLACEMENT FANGS

SEPARATE JAWS

Timber rattlesnake

85

populations by finding their easiest kills to be the weaker fishes, and this helps to keep the natural balance of nature by preventing overpopulation of the fish. Overpopulation in a body of water results in not enough food for all and a poor grade of fish. Predators weed out the weak.

Some folks cannot stand the sight of a snake. Some will kill any they see, poisonous or not. These feelings and actions are based in ignorance; actually, man derives much benefit from snakes. I shudder to think of how much our rat and mice population would increase without snakes.

As a naturalist, I assure you snakes are beneficial. I can only hope that more knowledge will make people aware of the necessity of proper balance in nature. Man frequently has upset this balance, and often the results have been tragic and costly.

Wildlife Specialists

Each species of life has particular features that enable it to live and reproduce.

The Poisonous Shrew. The short-tailed shrew —a common, mouselike animal found in burrows, fields and woods—is poisonous—and its poison causes paralysis. This poison is in the saliva of the animal and takes effect when its teeth open up its prey; the amount of poison secreted is small.

The shrew is the smallest of all mammals—

and is often mistaken for a mouse. However, examination of a shrew will show no external ears. It has very tiny eyes and a long, pointed nose. Its tail is usually much shorter than a mouse's, and it has five toes on the front feet. Most mice have only four.

No other mammal is more fierce than a shrew for its size. It eats anything from fish eggs and insects to birds, and it is even cannibalistic. It eats twice to three times its own weight each day. Ordinarily, its life span is little more than one year. Many meat-eating animals ignore it because it has a pair of glands that secrete a musky smell.

One species of shrew actually walks on the surface of water. This is made possible by a fringe of bristly hairs on its broad hind feet— the same principle that enables the insect called the "water strider," found on nearly all creeks and streams, to do the same.

The Katydid. This green, nocturnal insect, which lives in trees, has its ears out on its legs. They can be seen with the naked eye and appear as tiny slits. Its voice, as in many other insects, is produced not by vocal cords, but by external projections which are rubbed together, somewhat like producing a sound by rubbing your finger over an inflated balloon.

The katydid also has a special egg-laying device called an "ovipositor" (a term generally used for that organ in most female insects) which is a long, curved, bladelike instrument capable of slitting the edges of leaves wherein she often lays her flat, oval-shaped eggs.

The Bluffing Snake. An interesting snake is one I had in a cage while I painted its picture.

Shrew, hog-nosed snake, katydid

87

This "hog-nosed snake," apparently so named because of its turned-up nose, is commonly known as a "spreadhead" or "spreading viper." It is not really a viper, being completely nonpoisonous. It is found in most any place where there are toads, as they are on the diet of this snake. Its colors are tan and black with some variations—sometimes they are entirely black.

The actions of this snake disclose why it is called a "viper," but it is one of the biggest bluffers alive. When confronted by danger or a potential enemy, this harmless snake spreads its head and neck area to look every bit like a cobra, even raising its head like one. It will make false but very convincing moves to strike, always just short of the mark, hissing loudly all the while.

If all this pretense of ferocity fails to make the enemy retreat in terror, and the snake's bluff is called, it will roll over and give an excellent imitation of a dead snake. Not all do this, but most are such good actors that they may be picked up and no attempt whatever is made to "come to life."

Actually, the dumb thing, if turned right side up, will, in its complete attempt to feign death, roll right over again onto its back with its mouth agape and tongue hanging out on the ground. It will do so as many times as one wishes to turn it over. If the observer walks off and hides behind a tree, a few minutes of waiting will find the "dead snake" slyly raising its head to look around and, finding the danger gone, it will slither off.

Woodpecker Knocking Its Brains Out?

One of my favorite birds is the woodhen, or pileated woodpecker, as bird watchers call it. Once this loud-voiced fellow is seen, he is not soon forgotten. His size, alone, makes him a giant woodpecker compared with the others in our country except, of course, the nearly extinct ivory-billed woodpecker, which is found now only in primeval forests of the Deep South.

Eighteen inches in length, the woodhen is a handsome bird to watch—especially in flight, when the hidden pattern of white and black under the wing is exposed.

Woodpeckers in general are highly specialized in their development. They are insect eaters, but, unlike other insect-eating birds, most of the woodpecker species need not migrate far south in the fall to follow the food supply. They have the equipment that enables them to probe, dig, and rout out hibernating insects, grubs, bugs, spiders, and other foods from under the bark and inside trees the year around.

Hearing a woodpecker knocking on a tree, one wonders how such a terrific pounding fails to shake loose everything in the bird's head. If it were not for his highly specialized anatomy, it probably would!

The feet of woodpeckers, being different from most birds, can clasp the tree with two toes forward and two toes back, which provides a much stronger hold. They hop, not walk, up

Pileated woodpecker or woodhen

89

and down trees. Notice this action next time you watch a woodpecker.

With the powerful blows from the sharp beak, and the strong grip of its feet, the woodpecker necessarily requires extra support on the back end; it relies upon a special tail for this. Woodpeckers actually brace themselves, or sit down, on their tails for support. The tail is exceptionally stiff-shafted for this purpose and is curved downward to allow for extra pressure when the bird goes to work. When pressure is applied, the curve straightens but gives far more support than would be possible if the tail were straight to begin with.

The chisel-tipped bill of a woodpecker is perfect for cutting wood, and if you see one working you will notice that it expertly strikes the wood from varying angles to loosen the fibers of wood on the tree, as a woodsman works his axe. The tongue is fantastically long and has little barbs on the tip so that it can reach far into holes and "harpoon" morsels of food.

All this equipment, plus a great size and rich coloring add up to a mighty impressive bird. Woodpeckers are not often found away from the deep forests, although I have heard and seen them in some city parks. We are fortunate at our home to have a full woodland complement of them.

I think the title "woodhen," bestowed by rural folk, is a fitting one, for this loud "clucking" voice heard in the woods certainly does sound like a raucous hen, and it is heard more than the bird is seen.

A Bird Strokes Its Feathers—with an Ant!

The starling teetered and fell backward from having stepped on its own tail. The bird seemed dazed, as though it had had "one too many," but how would a starling get tipsy? Maybe it was having a fit of some kind. I was so intent upon the bird's strange behavior that I failed to attach any significance to the anthill upon which it cavorted.

Later, on reading an article in the *Audubon* magazine, I recalled the incident and became even more interested in what had happened on the anthill.

"Anting," which is the term applied to this mystery that still baffles students of birds, is not new to science. More than a hundred years ago, John J. Audubon observed and made notes of birds and their antics with the ants. Since then many have been intrigued by the peculiar habit, but few have actually witnessed it.

I wish that my own opportunity to observe it had not found me unprepared, through ignorance, to make the most of it. The information I have been able to find only further stimulates one to wonder, to speculate, to guess about explanations.

While performing this strange ritual, the bird is ecstatically entranced, to the point of being almost oblivious to its surroundings. Here is what happens during a typical anting:

The bird snatches up an ant in the tip of its bill, fans out its tail and wing, and brings the

Eagle and Osprey

Starling "anting"

Ray Harm

91

tail forward to the side of its body, alongside the legs. The ant is then rubbed along the tail feathers and the feathers of the wing. The bird uses additional ants for this rubbing action, eating them intermittently. Sometimes, used ants are cast away without being eaten. In the meantime, the bird becomes so absorbed that it will stagger, lose its balance, and even fall, as in the case I observed.

But why do birds contort themselves into this strange trancelike state? Why do they rub the ants along their tail and wing feathers?

Is anting merely a preening procedure? Is it a method of removing the formic acid found on ants, before eating the insects? Is the acid being transferred to the feathers to compensate for a deficiency? Is the ant rubbed in the plumage to rid the bird of parasites the ant may feed on?

Probably the person who has spent the most time in detailed study on this subject is the Canadian naturalist, Hance Roy Ivor. Through years of tests, experiments, and photography in his song-bird observatory, he has done a tremendous amount of fact sorting in efforts to track down the still-elusive answer to this puzzle.

Many birds will not ant at all, even when encouraged and given every opportunity. Some species will ant, but others of the same family classification will not. Removal of formic acid from the ant as a reason is unlikely, for many birds will gulp down mouthful after mouthful of ants without hesitation; also, seasonally dormant ants and those that do not excrete formic acid are used just as readily in anting.

Use of the high-speed camera has made possible the study in detail of anting procedures, and there is no evidence that the bird places ants in his plumage to attack parasites on the bird.

Bird lice are found only on the head or body of a bird and, in most cases, a bird will not permit a live ant on its body. The ant stroking is done only on the coarser outside wing and tail feathers.

My wife looked over my shoulder as I wrote this and quipped, "Maybe the friction heats up the ant and the bird likes its formic acid hot!" But sometimes the ants don't have formic acid, and sometimes the ants are not eaten!

What's the answer?

Your guess is as good as any.

*·AUTUMN

✍·Built-In Compass for Birds' Aerial Path

Above: scarlet tanager; below: American redstart

This winter, the beautiful and brilliantly colored scarlet tanager will travel all the way to Peru or Bolivia. The perky little redstart and the ovenbird are likely to be in the West Indies. The tiny and vivid yellow warbler flies all the way to Brazil to spend the winter months.

These are fantastically long trips for such small birds to make without maps or charts. How do they know when to start the trip, or what methods to use to navigate such great distances?

One theory—probably the most recent—is "celestial migration": the birds are guided by the stars and constellations.

Elaborate planetarium-type laboratory tests used in this study have brought out some rather convincing points. For instance, when the position of the constellations are changed, the birds changed their course accordingly.

It is true that most birds do migrate at night, but this theory fails to account for the many daytime migrants who sometimes fly thousands of miles with a high degree of navigational accuracy over large areas of water.

Some believe that the theory called "photoperiodism" explains how birds know when to begin their flight—that is, as the amount of daylight increases or decreases with the season, a stimulation takes place within the bird . . . a sort of alarm clock by which it departs.

Considering the amazing calendar arrivals and departures of some species, such as as the famous swallows of Capistrano, there is much to support this theory. Some birds, however, migrate from regions where the length of day does not change noticeably.

Bird migration will probably never be explained by a single answer, as most likely many factors apply to individual species.

Some facts about bird migration are widely agreed upon, at least in part, which give us some of the "why" answers. Surely the supply of food, the warmth and cold of seasonal changes, and the quest for greater nesting seclusion are likely reasons for migration.

Scientists know that seasonally there is an increased or decreased growth in the anatomical parts of birds and activity of the pituitary gland and sex glands. These changes are likely to "trigger" migratory trips to distant breeding grounds.

Other factors are generally accepted as to the "how" of migration for many birds. It seems obvious that landmarks are often used. Seacoasts are heavily relied upon, and rivers are followed. These points are strongly substantiated by our knowledge of the famous Mississippi, Atlantic, and Pacific "flyways" where millions of birds are observed following coasts and rivers annually.

The changing slant of the sun as the seasons progress may be another factor. It is likely that each bird has an acute awareness of the sun-arc in its home grounds. Many tests conducted with birds during migration have tended to show that this changing source of light is essential for many species as a navigational aid.

There are fantastic records of migrational flights by birds in respect to distance covered

and the time taken to do it. The remarkable Arctic tern, for example, breeds in the Arctic Circle, flies within a few months' time to the Antarctic (a distance of well over 10,000 miles), and returns in the same year.

A banded golden plover covered a distance of over 2,000 miles in two days over water. A lesser yellowlegs (one of the shore birds) is on record as having been banded in Massachusetts and killed six days later in the West Indies (a distance of over 1,900 miles), which was a trip covering more than 300 miles a day.

The Monarchs Take Off

On a recent trip from Kentucky to Cleveland, I broke the monotony of freeway driving by counting every monarch butterfly I sighted.

After logging a few, I realized that they were all crossing the highway from right to left, which was east to west. Of course. They were migrating—the date was October 3. All were heading in the same direction with the exception of six "questionables." My total count was sixty-four monarch butterflies.

One of the most interesting things about these beautiful insects is that they make these long migratory flights—as far as from Canada to Mexico—adding to the speculations of entomologists. A flight such as that is remarkable for a bird, but for a butterfly to make it and return is even more astonishing.

Only upon the milkweed plant does the fe-

Monarch butterfly. Above: caterpillar; below: adult emerged from pupa and drying its wings

96

male monarch lay her egg. I must add I have read that other acrid plants are sometimes used, but I do not know how well this is documented.

From the egg on the milkweed, the larva (caterpillar) hatches. After eating the eggshell, the larva begins its growth by eating from the plant on which it was hatched. During this process, as with the larva of so many insects, the caterpillar grows "too big for its britches," and its skin is shed several times before it changes into a pupa. In the pupal stage, that marvelous transition occurs wherein the final, complete change from young to adult is made. Later, it emerges an adult, golden-winged monarch.

The new adult, if it comes forth early in the summer, may live not much longer than time enough to fly farther north, mate, and secure its egg to another milkweed plant, leaving its offspring, or even the one from a later, third generation, to be the one to make the long migration to the south in the fall and return the following spring for another cycle. So far there is no evidence that an adult monarch lives long enough to make the trip twice.

Male monarchs can be distinguished from the females by the presence of a black spot on one of the veins of the hind wings. This spot contains scent glands which are brought into activity (to attract females) by a hair that can be extended for that purpose on each side of the body of the butterfly.

I have never seen a bird eat the monarch although I have watched birds experiment. Probably it has a bad taste because of the plants upon which it feeds. Enjoying a relatively safe life, it has a slow flight pattern.

Scientists are always much interested in getting reports back from tagged specimens so they can learn more about them. If you discover a monarch with a tag on the leading edge of its wing this year, the "tagger" will be grateful if you follow the directions on that tag. Someday you may have played a part in exploring the mystery of the migrating monarch.

A Mousetrap with Big Ears—the Hooting Barred Owl

On a moonless October night, when I was working for a cattle outfit in New Mexico, I was comfortably bedded down on the ground in my bedroll. My fire having long since died, I lay there in complete darkness, my thoughts wandering drowsily, when I was startled by a noise a short distance away.

I pressed the button on my flashlight. There in the light stood a whitish barn owl with a deer mouse divided between its bill and its claws. The owl had made its strike in total darkness.

When I was a boy, I had the common belief that owls could see in the dark, but later learning has corrected this misconception. It is true enough that the owl is better-equipped optically than man, for it can see more in less light. In this case, however, Mr. Barn Owl required no light at all—it was the ears, not the eyes, that were the range-finder.

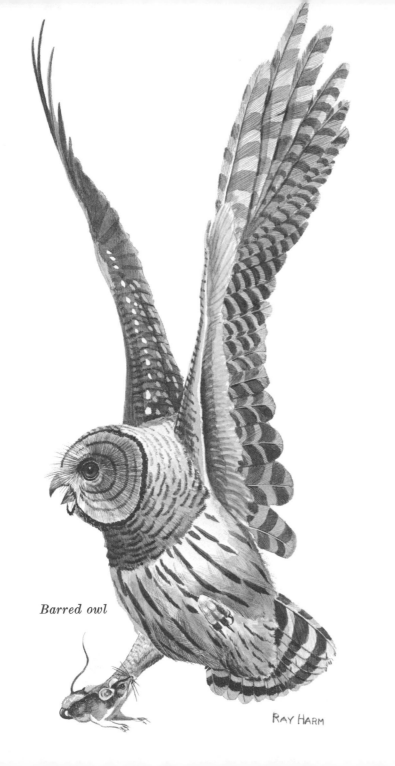

Barred owl

RAY HARM

Experimental tests conducted at Cornell University have shown that several species of owls are equipped with specialized ear anatomy that enables them to strike without the aid of light: Sound, of course, is the answer.

In Kentucky we have three birds with this additional hunting facility—the barred owl, the rarely seen long-eared owl, and the above-mentioned barn owl.

To me, the barred owl is the father of the "hooters," with a very loud, very full hoot. One of the most easily recognized owl voices, it almost invariably gives eight hoots to the call. The southern variety of this bird ends up its call with an "ooh-ah" sound (southerners call it the "you-all"), and we are likely to hear both variations of the call in this region.

For those of us who live in the woods, it is impossible to describe adequately the racket created when two or more barred owls get together for an evening bull session. The cackling, screaming, and witchlike laughing have to be heard to be believed.

The barred owl is a large bird, usually about twenty inches long, a brownish-gray color with bars running horizontally on its breast and streaked vertically on the belly. The head is large and round, and the eyes, which are brown, appear from a distance very black and somber. (Most owls have yellow eyes.)

Early in the spring this bird begins its nesting. It is known to use nests abandoned by other birds, such as other owls or the hawks, although a hollow tree usually serves its purpose. The young ones, numbering from two to four, are covered with fluffy, downy feathers. Their voracious appetites keep the parents busy.

Crows are natural enemies of the hawks and owls, probably because of nest raiding on the part of the owls and hawks—a crime of which the crow, himself, is not innocent. When the crows are raising a fuss back in the woods, it's almost sure that they've discovered an owl or a hawk, and are harassing the bird.

Farmers and hunters kill North American owls and hawks, considering them threats to the chicken coop and the game birds. Through the years, however, studies have proved that in nearly all species of owls, and hawks too, their average main diet consists heavily of mice and rats. The balance includes insects, spiders, frogs, and only occasionally a small bird.

I do not mean to say that certain hawks and owls—the Cooper's hawk and the great horned owl are examples—have not helped build such a reputation against the lot of them. At most, however, any damage done by these birds is well overbalanced by the good they do in keeping down the insect and rodent population.

The hunter and the farmer would do well to determine the true culprit in any case.

✐·Thin Legs Need Big Wings

Marsh birds have forms of specialization developed from their way of living that make them especially interesting. For instance, the great blue heron that flew to our lake the other morning was a large fellow with a wingspread of easily six feet.

This was a migrant bird, for I know of none that nest in Kentucky (except in the far western portion) ; we see them only in the early and latter part of the warm season.

When one of these big birds comes to our lake he first circles above it, each circle smaller than the previous one, then alights high in a tree to look the area over before dropping down to feed. To watch one come into the trees for a landing is to understand one of the reasons that this bird has developed such a great wingspread—so that he can come in slowly and carefully lest he injure those long spindly legs so necessary to him in fishing for aquatic food.

Great blues make many landings in trees, for they build their nests high in the trees (sometimes as high as one hundred feet), usually in rookeries among others of the same species.

The plumage of many such marsh birds includes a special type of feathers (called "powder down feathers") which grow continually from a bird's body and do not molt periodically as do the other feathers. They disintegrate at the tips, forming a powder that the bird uses in preening. It is believed that powder down feathers serve to help waterproof all the feathers and in general dress them up. If you could touch one of these birds you would find that the powder would rub off on your hands.

The tips of most bird feathers disintegrate in like manner to some extent, but not as much as powder downs. Marsh birds are not the only birds that grow powder down feathers—they are found on parrots, hawks, and some other birds, although usually growing more sparsely.

Some ornithologists believe that powder

Great blue heron

downs are more developed on the marsh birds because they may help to absorb oils, greases, or slippery skin coatings from the fish, frogs, and other prey of these birds, thereby acting as a protective agent for the body feathers.

✿·Woods Offer Food, Shelter, Fire— Even a Whistle

Without hesitation I would choose the American basswood (or linden) as my favorite tree. Many times in winter this tree has provided me with food. All I had to do was bend down the branches and pick from the tips two handfuls of the large red buds. They are entirely neutral in taste.

In the deep woods, where shelter was sometimes a problem when I was without equipment, large squares of bark peeled from the trunk of the tree have provided me with great shingles to build a very waterproof, snowproof, and windproof lean-to. For something to lash it together with, one has simply to peel long strips of the bark which is characteristic of this tree.

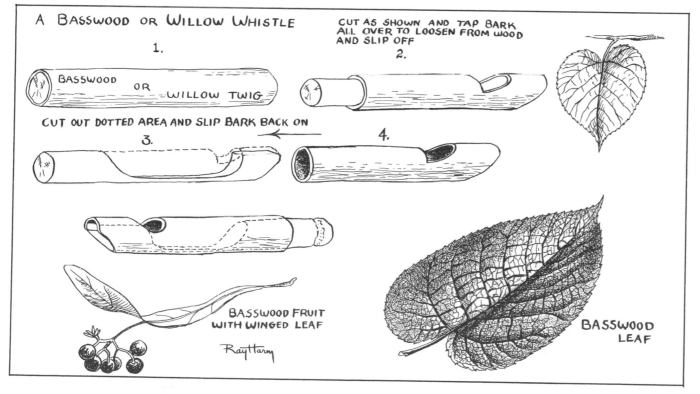

A BASSWOOD OR WILLOW WHISTLE

CUT AS SHOWN AND TAP BARK ALL OVER TO LOOSEN FROM WOOD AND SLIP OFF

1.

BASSWOOD OR WILLOW TWIG

CUT OUT DOTTED AREA AND SLIP BARK BACK ON

2.

3.

4.

BASSWOOD FRUIT WITH WINGED LEAF

Ray Harm

BASSWOOD LEAF

Top left: black walnuts; top right: hazelnuts; bottom left: butternuts; bottom right: hickory nuts

For warmth, the wood of the basswood is one of the preferred materials for fire-by-friction, and it is possible for a good woodsman to gather such equipment and make a fire within two hours.

Basswood inner bark makes string or rope that rivals our best Manila or sisal hemp.

In the spring, the tender leaves of the basswood are quite palatable, much like lettuce, and I often use a salad of basswood leaves and chopped cattail roots mixed with chopped ramps or Kentucky wild onion and a scattering of sour grass (sorrel) or sour clover for seasoning.

Spring is the best time for whistle-making from the basswood, when much moisture is under the bark. The bark is loosened from a selected piece of branch by tapping it with a closed pocket knife all around until it slips off easily.

Fall is the time of year when one does not need to carry food into the woods. At that time there are many ripening foods available, such as persimmons, pawpaws, haws, wild grapes, and honey-locust seeds, walnuts, beech nuts, butternuts, hazelnuts and even acorns and cattails.

Walnuts and butternuts must first have the outer green shell removed. This is a messy job, especially with the walnuts, because of the stain from the tannin in the covering. The fuzzy outer shell of the butternut, although sticky, is not as difficult to open. The meat of the butternut is delicious, but, as the name implies, is more buttery or oily than that of the walnut.

Hazelnuts grow on shrubs of that name. They

prefer bottomlands, benches, and thickets of rich soil. These are the wild form of the commercial "filberts." Few people recognize them while they are on the tree because of the strange husk surrounding them.

Nuts of the beech tree may be eaten raw, but also can provide either flour or beech-nut bread, or a good salad oil. Beech-nut flour is made simply by drying the nuts and grinding them into flour. The oil is made by grinding the nut meats, all the while adding small amounts of water until a thick paste is made. A strong cloth is needed in which to tie the paste. Pressure is then applied to force the oil through this bag.

Flour can be made also from acorns, those from the white oak preferred. They must be dried, and because of the bitterness of the raw nuts, they must be finely chopped and water run through them for a long time to remove the bitter taste. They are then spread out to dry again and ground into flour for many uses.

The buckeye is poisonous if eaten raw, but if the large seeds are roasted and peeled as one would peel chestnuts, then chopped fine and given the water treatment like that given the acorns, a good flour can be made.

Persimmon is primarily a southern tree but can be found in the East as far north as New England. Contrary to popular belief, a frost is not necessary before persimmons are ready to eat; when a persimmon ripens sufficiently to fall from the tree it will have lost its astringent, puckery taste.

Two ways to tell that they are ready are color, the red-pinkish frosted color they acquire

Persimmons

103

with maturity; and touch, they should be thoroughly soft. The only other criterion would be taste, and you'd soon learn the difference then!

My wife has her own recipe for persimmon pie. I have never tasted its equal anywhere, and with Carmella's permission I'd like to share it with you.

First, gather the persimmons and wash them in a colander. You will need about two quarts of persimmons to make the two heaping cups of pulp for the recipe.

Filling: 1 cup boiling water; 1 small package lemon gelatin; 1 heaping cup of persimmon pulp; 1 three-ounce package cream cheese; ½ cup granulated sugar; ¼ cup chopped walnuts (or hickory); 1 small can evaporated milk (cold).

Crust: 1¾ cups fine graham cracker crumbs; ⅓ stick of butter.

Glaze: 1 cup persimmon pulp; 1 cup water; 11½ tablespoons cornstarch; ½ cup sugar.

Step by step:

1. Mix the gelatin with the boiling water and set to cool in refrigerator until it thickens.

2. To make the crust, melt the butter and mix with graham cracker crumbs. Line a 9-inch glass pie pan by pressing this mixture firmly into it.

3. Squeeze the persimmons through a ricer into a bowl. This is to separate the pulp from the seeds.

4. Blend the cream cheese and sugar and add one heaping cup of persimmon pulp.

5. Add the partially set gelatin and chopped nuts.

6. Whip the cold evaporated milk until stiff, and fold into mixture.

7. Pour mixture into pie crust and set to chill.

8. To make glaze, use glass or stainless steel double boiler. In it, put the remaining cup of persimmon pulp, add cup of water and cook two minutes.

9. Mix sugar and cornstarch and stir into hot persimmon. Bring to slow boil and stir until mixture thickens.

10. Remove from heat and cool to room temperature.

11. Pour glaze over chilled persimmon pie.

12. Chill entire pie for two hours.

Then go to it!

The proper time to eat pawpaws is when the skin has turned to a nice yellowish brown. When the pulp can be squeezed right out of the skin into the mouth, it is ripe and ready to eat.

The tree itself is only about fifteen feet tall and grows in the open as well as in the shade. On the knobs where I live, the pawpaw is commonly found on moist north slopes along spring runs and creeks.

The leaves, also, are readily identified, even from a distance. It is a good idea, in one's wandering, to peg down the location of such trees and watch them for the appearance of the fruit later on, usually around the first of September.

Pawpaws can be used in a variety of ways, as a pie filling and in ice-cream making. Surprisingly, considering their own natural sweetness, they often are eaten with cream and sugar. A custard may be made by mashing the ripe, pulpy fruit and mixing a little cream into it until the desired custard consistency is attained.

I have seldom eaten pawpaws without taking the large slippery seeds and heeling them into the ground for the future.

Some folks say that a taste for pawpaws has to be acquired, but I guess I had a built-in taste for them when I was born.

Looking for Blight-Resistant Chestnuts

My good friend and neighbor Cletis Weller, who is naturalist for the State parks, was hap-pily surprised recently when he came upon a very special tree back in the woods.

It is an American chestnut tree, burrs and all. About seven inches in diameter, it stands thirty-five feet tall, and, from all outward appear-ances, seems the picture of health! Because of the scourge of the chestnut blight, we shall keep watch on the young tree in hope that this off-spring of the once great American tree will have built up a blight immunity.

The disease that was literally to wipe out entire forests of this giant tree, with its deli-cious sweet nut, was discovered in New York City at about the turn of the century. It was found to be a fungus that attacks the living layer of cambium beneath the bark. Because it

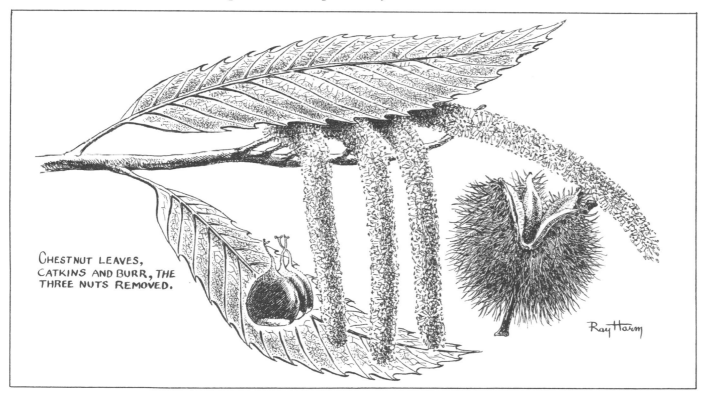

CHESTNUT LEAVES, CATKINS AND BURR, THE THREE NUTS REMOVED.

Ray Harm

is a fungus, it releases, by the thousands, spores that ride the wind and the bodies of tree-dwelling insects.

In spite of the wide-sweeping devastation of this blight for some sixty years, a surprising number of chestnut trees eight inches or more in diameter are being reported to the U.S. Forest Service. They are keeping these trees under surveillance and are asking people who report the tree to send samples of the burr, leaf, twig, and nut for positive identification.

Later, a request is sent for specific cutting for the purpose of grafting onto the cultivated, blight-resistant Chinese chestnut. From this graft, they hope to produce a blight-resistant American chestnut. It is hoped that by now, long after the height of the blight, some of the young trees, such as the one Cletis found, may have built up an immunity.

There is one discouraging thought: it makes some sense that because the blight has pretty much eliminated the mature trees, the fungus has left itself so little to feed upon that it may be abated only temporarily in the areas where these new trees are found. On the other hand, trees have built up immunities to blights before, and the Forest Service people are hoping that somewhere these new young chestnut trees have done just that.

WINTER

Foreground: Male purple finch
Background: Female purple finch

✒·Bedding Down for Winter

Breathing was hardly perceptible. The blood circulation seemingly had stopped. Body and limbs were stiffly cold, body temperature was down to 40 degrees. Does this sound like a real crisis? Not at all. Woodchucks undergo this condition every winter.

Most of our animals bed down for the winter. Much change takes place in animal life in preparation for cold weather. The fur bearers feed themselves fat and grow long hair. The reptiles become stiffer with each colder day and find holes or dens in which to spend the winter in a state of hibernation. Amphibians dig deep into the mud below lakes and ponds.

Winter brings about new aspects of specialization in many forms of animal life. For example, the ruffed grouse develops a pair of snowshoes by growing extra comblike protrusions from both sides of all its toes. The end of the fox's tail becomes much bushier; he uses this to protect his nose from frostbite when he curls up to sleep. The weasel changes its brown fur to a pure white ermine coat for winter camouflage.

How is a frog able to breathe while buried in the mud below the water all winter long? As with most hibernators, the body does not demand a great deal of air or food during its long sleep. Nature enables the frog to reduce its entire body operation radically.

In this dormant stage it can subsist on the very smallest amount of food from its own fat. Attempting to breathe through the nose would fill its lungs with mud and, of course, it couldn't hold its breath all winter, so a different breath-

ing process takes over in the winter.

The frog breathes through its skin, taking oxygen from the air in the mud surrounding its body. In minute amounts, air is distributed to the system. Subsistence is possible in this condition only because, during hibernation, the requirements for body functions and metabolism are so greatly reduced.

Actually, true hibernation is a rare thing. In the most technical sense it is a condition wherein body activity is so reduced that, for example, in a bat, an embryo will cease to grow, along with the parent, for the duration of hibernation.

There are records of certain foreign lungfish that were discovered in dried balls of mud in an area that was known not to have had water in it for years (in one case as long as fifty years) and after immersion in water, the lungfish awoke from this torpid state and regained normal activity.

Sounds like a tall story, doesn't it? Surely, in this instance, truth is stranger than fiction.

✎·Quick Heartbeat Warms Birds

At the time this is being written, the temperature outside is 10 degrees below zero—extraordinarily cold for Kentucky! From where I sit in my studio I can see an assortment of birds picking seed from the snow outside.

There are, as one might expect, thirty to forty snowbirds (slate-colored juncos), several cardinals, two of those large impressively marked birds called "fox sparrows," a few white-throated sparrows, and one song sparrow. Kentucky cardinals are picking corn from the cobs that are spiked to the trees, and, of course, the ever-present jays are all about.

At the other side of the house, on our kitchen-window platform feeder, are many purple finches, filling their crops with sunflower seeds. They are joined by Carolina chickadees and tufted titmice.

A bedroom overhangs the entrance to the rear of our house, where the protected ground below is bare, and dry fall leaves have blown up against the foundation. A brown thrasher is scratching leaves aside. (The brown thrasher is of special interest, of course, because that bird is seldom in Kentucky during the wintertime.) A couple of towhees are doing the same, along with more snowbirds and redbirds. One yellow-hammer and two sapsuckers are feeding on some grapes I scattered on the ground.

Earlier this morning Carmella called me to the kitchen window and pointed out several evening grosbeaks (another beautifully colored bird that sometimes visits Kentucky in the winter).

Last night a female mourning dove settled down in the dry leaves against the foundation of the house, under the extended bedroom, and went to sleep. When our son Hap took his sled out to try one last hill just before dark, she flew off in fright, but as I watched Hap go he had walked little more than fifty yards when the dove flew back to the leaves, fluffed up, and settled down like a hen coming back to her eggs.

Fox sparrow

111

This morning I flicked on the light over the entrance to see if she was still there, and, sure enough, there in the same spot sat a large puff of olive russet feathers with a blinking eye on one side and a tail on the other. A few feet away sat a cottontail rabbit eating the last of the grapes I had scattered on the ground.

It seems impossible that the tiny blood vessels in a small bird could keep it from freezing in such cold temperatures. A comparable sliver of water would freeze immediately, and the circulation in my own fingers falls short of being as effective!

But the heart of a bird beats much faster than ours—a bird's circulation and metabolism are very fast. That is why birds can die so quickly of starvation or a little poison spray on or in their food.

✒ · Bird-Feeding—a Full-Time Chore

The feeding and care of wild birds can be an arduous undertaking; they must be fed very frequently because of their high rate of metabolism and the ravenous appetite that goes with it.

First of all, having a bird feeder can be a *bad* thing if the birds are not fed regularly. Feeders sometimes attract much larger numbers of birds to an area than the area alone could support. It is essential, then, that feeding be dependable, especially during winter months. Withdrawal of feed could be fatal to many of the highly-keyed small birds who might wait

A home feeder

around to be fed until it could be too late for them to gather enough food on their own.

The necessity of feeder upkeep applies also to summertime feeding when fatalities could be the young of the adult nesting birds who could not compete in such a crowded area for food off the land.

Though not as critical in rural areas as with city feeders, this point should always be considered. If for some reason it is absolutely necessary to stop feeding, it should be tapered off gradually.

A summer feeder has more bird varieties around, and it can be especially entertaining when adult birds bring their young to the feeder for the first time.

Young birds must have the right kind of food to safeguard their health. Of course, if one can learn what the parent birds of a given species feed their young, it helps. Sometimes the food given to young birds is *not* what the parents would eat. The diet may gradually change to fit the bird's ability to swallow or digest as the nestling grows older.

As to bird food itself, I provide only three essential foods at my feeders, separately, which keeps the birds separated accordingly. I feed only sunflower seeds on my window feeders, scratch and assorted feed on the ground below, and to the side and somewhat above, I attach my suet to the trees. This tends to keep the juncos, finches, sparrows, and jays on the ground, permitting nuthatches, chickadees, titmice, cardinals, and grosbeaks at the sunflower seeds on the window feeders. Some eat at both places, of course, but the majority will separate.

The suet in the trees attracts primarily woodpeckers and nuthatches, but others come there too. I like to sprinkle sand and gravel among the scratch feeder; the seed eaters, particularly the juncos, appreciate the roughage, especially in the winter if snows are heavy.

Raisins without chemicals added, small pieces of apple, raw peanuts, and other natural seeds are good foods for birds. I am convinced that bread is not good for wild birds because it is too far removed from their wild food. I feel the same about peanut butter, which has been under investigation as a cause of mortality among chickadees in particular. It seems they may have trouble swallowing it.

In any case it is a good idea to feed wild things, as nearly as possible, what they would get in the wild.

Mistletoe Provides Color, Gaiety— and Money

My dictionary, turned to the word "mistletoe," says in part, "A sprig of such a plant, hung as a Christmas decoration; men are by custom privileged to kiss women standing under it." I suppose there is a history about the origin of this custom; I don't know it, but it should be interesting.

The scientific name for mistletoe is "phoradendron" which, when translated from the Greek, means "tree robber." That is a pretty good name; mistletoe is a parasite, living upon

Mistletoe

several varieties of trees, although it does contain chlorophyll.

A perennial woody shrub, the mistletoe that grows in our Southeast is the familiar species used during the Christmas holidays. Being parasitic, it needs no soil in which to grow. It has an interesting root system that grows through the bark of the host tree, penetrating into the sapwood to live from the tree's life blood, so to speak.

After the trees have lost their leaves in the fall, the yellowish-green clumps of mistletoe are easily seen. It would be unusual to drive a mile on a Kentucky highway without spotting several clumps of it high in the trees. They form clusters, on the average of a foot across.

The fruit, which appears in November, is a pearl-white berry growing in bunches from the branches.

Along with fun and holiday spirit under the mistletoe, it should be remembered that mistletoe is poisonous to eat. Although earlier books on medicinal herbs actually recommended it as a stimulant, at least one death is officially on record, the result of drinking a brew made from the leaves. Although the proportion of the recommended mixture may not be enough to harm a healthy person, it certainly does not allow for individual sensitivity.

Mistletoe often is found growing high, near the tops of trees and far out on branches. These trees are all deciduous trees, such as maple, elm, hickory, and locust. I have never seen mistletoe on an evergreen tree.

In spite of its frequently being inaccessible, many a country boy has earned extra money by collecting and selling sacks of mistletoe for the local Christmas market.

Most of the year this plant gets no attention at all; then suddenly, for the holidays, it becomes the belle of the ball.

✐·The Walking Fern of Wintry Woods

Winter woods are characterized by a lack of color and the cold, bare appearance of the leafless oaks and maples. A second look, however, will disclose how little we sometimes see and will reveal surprises in color from sumac fruit, bittersweet, holly trees, pine and cedars, mosses and ferns, to mention a few. Of the last, the walking fern, native to Kentucky, does, in a way, walk.

Growing chiefly on limestone, the walking fern is easily recognized by clusters of tapered, richly-green leaves which will often grow ten inches or more in length. It usually grows out of soil and mosses that are also found on the limestone rocks. The long, arrow-shaped leaf does not fit into the common concept of how ferns are supposed to look, with their lacy, deeply-lobed leaves.

Fern it is, though, and generally it fits into the same classification as other ferns very well. Of the two species of walking ferns found in the entire world, one is American, the other is Asian.

This interesting plant arches gracefully, and when the downward curving tip of the leaf comes in contact with the ground it may take root and grow off in another direction, take root again, and so on, until the patch is quite large. This is the reason for its title, and it is a welcome crop of greenery on a cold winter day in Kentucky.

Another source of green in our winter woods is the Christmas fern, not as lacy as some, but not as coarse as others.

It is probably our best-known fern, is widely distributed, and is used as a Christmas decoration by country folk because of its evergreen quality. It is known best for the similarity of each "pinna" (leaf) to a Christmas stocking (see inset).

This plant grows throughout the woods and on rocky hillsides all over Kentucky. There are many variations of the species that are strikingly different in outline, but the Christmas stocking pinnae are recognizable in all of them.

I have often eaten fern fiddleheads, especially the curled fronds of the cinnamon fern. These can be cooked or the hearts can be used for

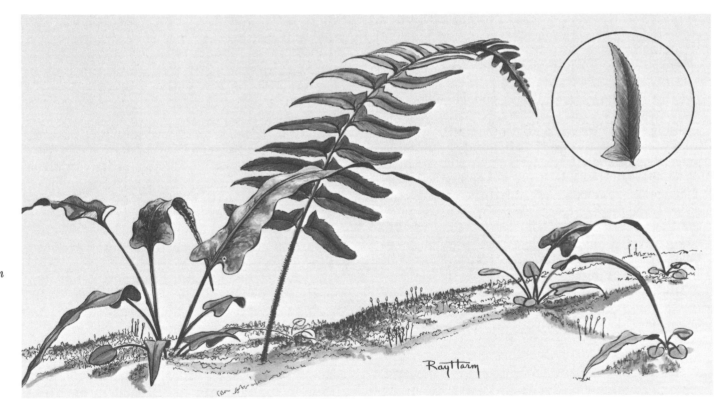

Walking fern

116

making a fern salad. I just eat them raw in the woods.

The bracken fern can be used as a cooked vegetable. It tastes much like asparagus, I am told, or like a spring green.

Always leave a few fiddleheads in each group to insure that next year the ferns there will still continue growing.

Feeding Young Owls Is No Small Task

Last spring, a friend called from Bardstown to tell my wife about a family of screech owls in trouble near her home. The owls were very young and out of the nest hole. When returned to it, they would not stay put.

What with the neighborhood children, dogs, cats, and automobiles, it didn't appear that the three downy owlets had much of a chance for survival; so my wife drove into town and picked them up.

Back home again, Carmella and our son Hap constructed a large cage for them on our sun deck. Hap then assumed the responsibility of gathering food for the young birds.

They were small and wouldn't eat much (so he figured!). They needed insects, so for nighttime he arranged a light bulb outside with a bottle trap below, into which the attracted insects dropped after striking the light.

As the weeks passed and the owls grew larger, so did their appetites. Two more light

Young screech owl

117

traps were needed and still the owls ate every-thing offered. Hap really had to hop to supply food for them; he gained a healthy respect for a parent owl's duties.

Those birds consumed a mountain of moths, May beetles, woodland roaches, stag beetles, and a host of others. As they grew still larger, Hap met the challenge and augmented the daily food supply by catching grasshoppers and other diurnal insects. They certainly kept Hap going aplenty, but he kept their larder full; the owls fared well, but I think Hap slimmed down some.

We started training them to "hunt" by releasing live insects into the cage. The owls pounced upon their prey quite instinctively. It was interesting to watch their hunting methods improve day by day. We did not handle them.

To take some pressure off Hap, we offered them raw liver occasionally. Now and then we released live-trapped mice onto the leafy floor of their cage. In that way the owlets were exposed, at least partially, to hunting requirements in the wild.

When they became old enough we took them to the edge of the woods, on an upland field near home, and released them.

It's winter now, and they are still around. We have heard them call occasionally. Recently a sound at a living room window caught our attention; there was one of our owls, his chest feathers pressed flat against our windowpane, peering inside with his round yellow eyes.

"Bet he's looking for me!" said Hap.

The Unappealing Turkey Vulture

The turkey vulture, along with its relative the black vulture, is sometimes called the "garbage can of the South." Because the carrion eaters remove many animals killed on southern highways, and much of the garbage in the streets and alleys, they are protected by law.

By human standards, the bird is repulsive. In addition to its feeding upon decaying animal matter and garbage, it regurgitates a horrible substance when frightened. Its head is without feathers; on the ground, the vulture is awkward and the picture of ugliness.

Ironically, when airborne, this ugly creature turns into a form of beauty and grace, carried on a sloping five- or six-foot wingspread. Turkey vultures soar for hours without a single flap of wings, borne by the ever rising air of the hills and hollows to heights high above the knobs, often swooping low over the treetops in search of food.

Most bird books attribute this bird's ability to locate hard-to-find prey to its exceptionally keen eyesight. From Audubon to modern times, there has been great disagreement among ornithologists on how this bird locates the food it eats (for in dead material there is no movement to attract attention). Is it by smell or sight?

Indeed, most vultures do have extraordinary sight. Very recent extensive field tests conducted by Dr. Kenneth E. Stager, and described by him in his paper published by the Los

Turkey vulture. Birds in flight—left: turkey vulture; right: black vulture

Angeles County Museum, have just about settled any arguments about the mode of food discovery by the North American turkey vulture. The olfactory sense pretty conclusively proved to be the answer.

The bird is at a disadvantage on the ground with such a large wingspread, and it usually has difficulty taking off. I saw a vulture lose its life on an interstate highway near Louisville last summer because of this. It had been feeding on a dead, smashed box turtle when an approaching automobile scared it into attempting flight. A downwind takeoff was impossible. The necessary upwind direction led directly into the path of the oncoming car. The large bird simply could not gain altitude quickly enough to escape.

Turkey vultures build no nests as such, but lay their eggs right on the ground under cliffs or in hollow logs, rock cavities, or hollow stumps, usually at higher elevations. It is a smelly home they live in because the young ones regurgitate indigestible material on the spot, not a very neat situation.

In the spring and summer, try to distinguish the large turkey vulture from the black vulture over any part of Kentucky. The main differences in these common birds are: the black vulture flaps its wings frequently—the turkey vulture does not. The adult turkey vulture has a red, naked head—the black vulture is gray or black-headed.

Two other determining features in field identification between the two species are the difference in light areas shown on the under part of the wings, and the length of the tails.

✒ · "Rabbit Ice" Grows Three Feet Up

An interesting phenomenon brought about by cold weather is a strange formation called "rabbit ice." It forms around the base of a wild plant called by several names: "white ironweed," "crownbeard," or "frostweed"; the scientific name is *verbesina virginica*.

When the first hard frost arrives, while the plant is still growing and full of sap, these ice formations manifest themselves in unusual proportions and size, sometimes as tall as three feet up the stem. As seasonal growth wanes, however, there is less and less sap produced. Consequently, ice formations are less evident as winter progresses.

The host plant itself is a tall one, often growing six feet or more. The dead stalk in the winter, or the living stalk in the summer and fall, is easily recognized by its height and heavily winged stem.

On a cold, frosty morning in late fall or winter, these glistening white "growths" of ice have an eerie and bizarre appearance, especially when seen against a snowless background.

Sometimes, large areas of bottomlands or fields are covered by these knee-high ice formations.

I can only guess about the cause of rabbit ice, and certainly can provide no technical answers. It seems likely that the plant has something special in its sap or its makeup that allows the nippy temperatures to freeze the sap so rapidly in such a way.

Initially, the outer skin of the plant bursts open when the sap beneath it freezes and expands. It would seem that more liquid sap is sent from the roots to the freezing area continually, where it, too, freezes and expands, pushing that which is already frozen on the outside farther and farther away from the stem, thus creating the strange white cluster of frozen curl around the stem.

I watched rabbit ice being formed one evening as a sharp drop in temperature caused flaky, wafer-like sheets of the curling ice to push out of the white ironweed. In less than an hour it emerged more than a half-inch from the stem of the plant.

The reason for the name "rabbit ice" is beyond me, except that the plant often grows in brushy areas where rabbits may be found.

120

"Rabbit ice"

121

✍·Fence Lizard a Familiar Sight

I saw my first fence lizard this year on February 18. He was basking on the sunny side of a large dogwood tree.

The "pine lizard" (as the fence lizard is commonly called) should be familiar to all Kentuckians who have spent even a little time in the woods. He is often heard before he is seen because, as he scampers swiftly up a tree (usually squirrel fashion on the opposite side), he pays no mind to making noise, which is considerable for his size. These lizards usually run up the tree only a short distance, but this distance is lengthened rapidly if one moves closer.

Fence lizards are very keen of sight, but if a person sits quite still for a short while, they do not seem to mind the presence of man at all and will go about their business unless a slight move by the observer sends them scampering again.

Often they will lie upon a perch or an elevated jut of rock, and do "push-ups" for you. I'm not sure of what this indicates, but I have watched them do these "push-ups" both solo and when confronted by another lizard. It could be a maneuver that enables the animal to change its visual perspective, or focus, on whatever subject it may be concerned with; or possibly it is some sort of hostile display.

The male pine lizard can be identified by the iridescent blue patches on his belly and lower throat, when he raises his head. The iridescence is lessened, of course, in the absence of sunshine, but nevertheless he is colorful. It may also be less just before the animal sheds his skin.

The female appears to have more distinctly

Fence lizard

marked patterns on her back than the male. Both may be brown or gray (or both colors), and their markings are a wavy pattern on the upper side.

They hibernate during the winter and come forth each spring, to take up housekeeping. Later, usually in June or July, the female lizard lays a number of eggs in a hole she digs in the ground for that purpose, then covers them and forgets about them completely. Nature does the rest, and a dozen or more little ones may dig themselves out of the hole late in the summer, ready to fend for themselves.

These lizards will grow in length to seven inches, and not infrequently are seen with only stubs left for tails. This is likely evidence of a fight with another lizard, or possibly a near miss by a predator. They grow new tails, however, which usually fall short of their original length.

Collectively these lizards contribute greatly toward the balance of nature, both by eating insects and serving as food for other wildlife. They move very swiftly (hence their other common name, "brown swift") and are a familiar sight wherever there are woods.

Wild Deer in the Woods

Buck rubs are not an uncommon sight in the woods, but they are commonly misinterpreted by man. The deer is *not* rubbing the shedding summer velvet from his antlers.

In Kentucky, by the time bucks start their antler rubbing, the velvet is usually gone. In fact, by mid-December, so are many antlers, many mature bucks having already shed them. Just the other day I saw one through my field glasses showing little evidence that the shedding had even been very recent, for the new skin was already nearly grown over where each antler had been.

This buck will be without antlers until April or May, when new ones begin growing into fuzzy, velvet-covered antlers that are comparatively soft, filled with sensitive nerves and plenty of blood in circulation.

By September the antlers will be fully grown and hardened. The velvet covering will then be shed by its own process of drying, cracking apart and falling off, usually in less than a day's time.

Shortly afterward, the buck will become restless because the mating season approaches. All summer he has eaten well until, in prime condition by October, with his handsome new antlers, he is ready for a little sport. Like other males he starts to roam the woods in search of other deer.

A buck rub is simply a sign of this period when a buck, anticipating the mating time, which also brings on fights with other bucks, uses the sapling to practice and strengthen himself into condition for meeting other males.

To me, few animals are as impressive to see in the woods as deer. To behold a thick-necked buck on the alert brings a heart-pounding moment, no matter how often one is privileged to see it, and I make that statement with firsthand knowledge, for I have seen many.

Equally pleasurable is the sight of a fawn.

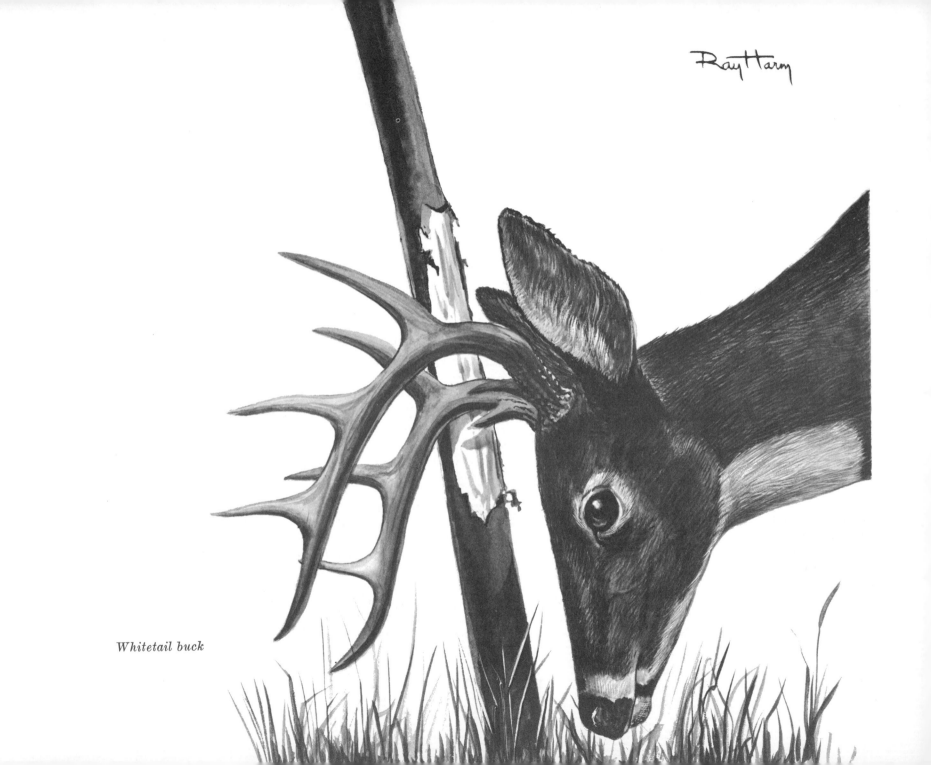

Ray Harm

Whitetail buck

One of the most treasured memories of my life is the time I came upon a doe late one afternoon giving birth to her fawns. She was in a stand of large white pine trees which I knew had formerly been one of the favorite daylight bed grounds of the local deer. She had already dropped one, and the second was in progress. It was summer, and it was hot. The doe's tongue seemed to be a foot long as the animal stretched out upon the thick soft bed of pine needles.

After the births I wanted to help chase the deer flies from the heads of all three—the doe's nose was practically raw from previous bites already—but of course I stayed put.

Deer are not normally grass eaters. They browse on twigs, buds, leaves, acorns, and berries. They do go to alfalfa readily, however, and, during lean days, will eat hay. I have noticed that near my home the deer feed in the winter on cedar, smilax, or greenbrier and twigs and buds of maple.

In the summer they eat wild hydrangea, greenbrier, wild grape leaves, and strawberry bush. Many other foods too numerous to mention here are included in their diet, which varies, depending upon the locale.

I am very disturbed that so many deer are run down by loose, wandering packs of domestic dogs and hounds. Few people realize that, although a deer is quite fast in a sprint, he is short of wind on a run. Very likely a man could run one down if he could keep one on the level and in the open. Their nature is not conducive to having strong wind and stamina. To see a pack of dogs pull down a deer, tear it up, and leave it lying is a revolting thing.

Friendly, Acrobatic Chickadee— Everyone's Favorite

I looked over my shoulder toward the familiar sound of a small bird's wings and saw a chickadee light upon a branch. In its mouth was a huge cluster of wood chips and scrapings. He stood there a moment, and then, with an audible "puff" and a snap of his head, sent the cluster of chips scattering like a miniature explosion.

He flew down and disappeared into a tiny hole he had made in the decaying stump of a tulip tree sapling that had broken off about four feet above the ground. The chickadee had started to dig the hole for his nest in the soft wood about six inches below the break.

Within half an hour I watched this tiny bird make many similar trips, each time repeating the process of scattering the punky wood it was digging out of the tree. At one time, when the bird had disappeared into the hole, I quickly and quietly stepped over to the dead sapling and stood there, only inches away, to see what would happen.

The chickadee appeared at the entrance again, mouth full, and, seeming not to mind my presence, it flew to a lofty perch and scattered its wood chips. When it returned to the next hole, it actually alighted upon the sleeve of my shirt first, then flitted over to the hole and disappeared into it for some more digging.

The chickadee is a very popular, if not the most popular, bird wherever people put out bird feeders. Easily attracted near homes, this acrobatic often upside-down little bird grasps a

Chickadee

sunflower seed with its toes, pins it to the perch, and hammers away vigorously with its bill to open the shell of the seed. For its size, only four and a half inches, it consumes a fantastic amount of insects and vegetable matter.

Once, when one flew against our window and lay stunned in the snow, I went out to pick it up and made the mistake of handling it by its tail feathers. To my dismay, they all came loose in my hand. The bird recovered and flew off minus its entire tail, although its flight left something to be desired. In just a short week it had a new tail growing back, but the new feathers were pure white; apparently the pigmentation of the skin was damaged when the feathers pulled out.

For the remainder of the winter our feeder was host to a white-tailed chickadee, which provided excellent opportunity for me to observe its feeding habits—how much it ate, what times of the day it fed heaviest, and how often it returned to the feeder. The spring feather molt must have found the skin damage repaired, because we no longer spotted our white-tailed bird.

In the woods, I have had chickadees alight upon my person when several were feeding close to the ground, and at the feeder they can be fed by hand, although this takes much patience on the part of the human being.

In the North and Northeast of our country, the black-capped chickadee is most common. (The cap is brown in northern New England and Canada.) In the Southeast we have the Carolina chickadee, which is almost identical to the black-capped, but smaller. The West has the greatest number of varieties, including the mountain chickadee with a white stripe over the eye. Wherever found, there little titmice have in common very active, acrobatic, insect-hunting lives, and derive their name from their song, ''chickadee.''

The Yellow on Yellow-Bellied Sapsucker

The yellow-bellied sapsucker? What a classic bird-watcher name!

Strangely, however, a yellow-colored belly is seldom mentioned in the bird books as one of the identification marks to look for on this bird. This is understandable because there isn't much yellow on the belly of a yellow-bellied sapsucker!

It is an interesting bird, and there are several things about this woodpecker that set him apart from the others.

Ornithologists have made several studies showing strong evidence that some of the beliefs about the bird may not have much validity. For example, it has been thought that the rows of holes the sapsucker makes in the trees will result in the death of the tree.

Not true, except perhaps very rarely.

Also, in some areas it is generally believed that the drilling of these holes by sapsuckers is purely for the purpose of attracting insects to the sweet sap flow where the bird can feed upon them.

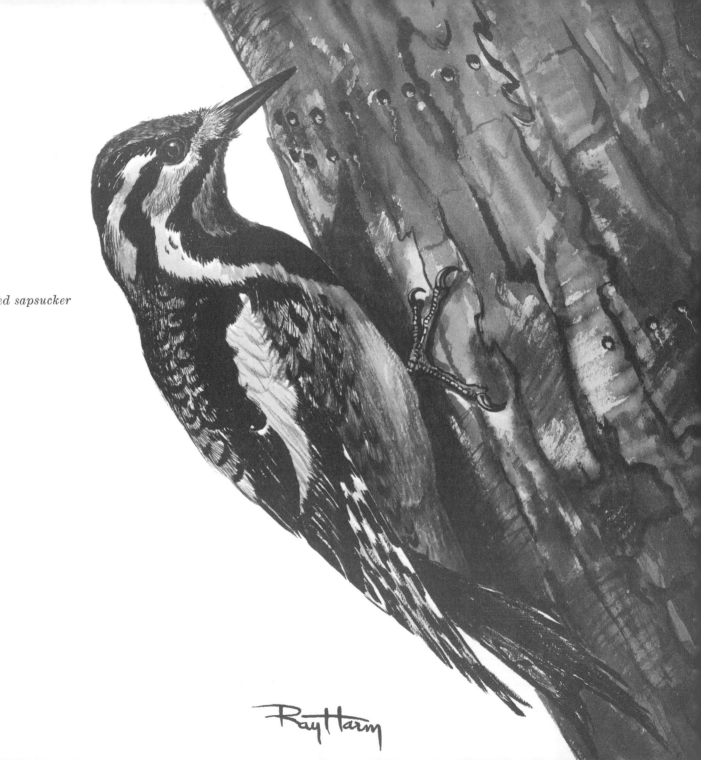

Yellow-bellied sapsucker

128

Also not true, although naturally the bird will take advantage of the fact that the sweet sap of many trees does attract a variety of insects. (It also attracts some other birds and even mammals.) But the sapsuckers do eat the sap from trees, and the primary purpose of the bird in drilling these rows of holes in trees is to get sap.

Lawrence Kilham, an ornithologist in New Hampshire, brought out some interesting conclusions in a paper he write for *The Auk,* a journal of ornithology. The paper was the result of a study he made of this species in its nesting area.

Kilham observed that when sapsuckers were feeding upon the sap, they paid little attention to nearby insects; and when they did feed upon insects, they usually caught them by other methods.

It seems that when a tree is wounded, it may send sap with additional nutrients to the wounded area to repair the damage, the sapsucker thereby benefiting by getting sap with additional sugars in it. That could be why sapsuckers often work a tree that has been skinned or wounded in some manner, perhaps by a falling tree, in preference to a healthy tree.

The adult birds are clear-cut in pattern, but the young birds are spotted and mottled with black, washed with a tinge of yellow in varying degrees. As with most woodpeckers, the male has a good deal more red on his head than does the female sapsucker. All ages of sapsuckers, however, are easily recognized by the long white wing patch they display.

This woodpecker is a migrant through Kentucky, but it is not uncommon to have it winter with us. Folks in the South often refer to it as the "Yankee woodpecker" because, like some other northerners, it is seen by southerners only in the winter.

Purple Finch, a Raspberry Powder Puff

The eastern purple finch is a bird unfamiliar to most Kentuckians and, for that matter, to most Americans; but the chances are good for getting a look at this handsome little bird if a sharp eye is kept open in the wintertime any place in the eastern United States.

In the spring and summer, the nesting range of the purple finch is in Canada and as far south as North Dakota, northern Illinois, and on over to Long Island. When the weather starts cooling, the immature and adult birds start their migratory trip south, to scatter in small flocks and spend the winter over the eastern states.

I am sure this bird is often overlooked because of similarity in size to the sparrows, and because the female finch is quite like a sparrow in color. Close inspection, however, will reveal a much heavier bill, dark brown streaking on her sides, and a heavy marking of the same color on her jaw.

The male bird is notable for his outstanding

Eastern purple finch

Ray Harm

color, and I agree with the commonly used "raspberry" describing it. He is liberally washed with "red raspberry stain" on his entire front half, and if his wings happen to relax, as they often do while he is feeding, they reveal an even brighter raspberry color on his rump.

The earliest I saw one in Kentucky was on November 8, when a few spooked out from a pine thicket in the Bernheim Forest. These were early migrants—I saw no numbers around until later on in December when these first ones probably had gone on farther south. In January, a cold snap brought a small flock of them in to feed regularly upon the sunflower seeds we offer at our window feeder.

To watch them is entertaining. The female bird seems more aggressive while feeding; if another bird comes too close, she will sometimes drop her wings to the ground and vibrate them rapidly while opening her mouth wide. This hostile display usually causes the intruder (male or female) to give ground readily.

Late in the morning, after feeding, the finches sometimes perch along branches in nearby trees, fluffed up like airy balls of feathers, insulating themselves against the cold. In this manner, the males look like round raspberry powder puffs growing from the branches. At night they roost in a small stand of Virginia pine on a bench of land below our house.

In the early days of our country, purple finches, along with cardinals and other colorful songbirds, were kept as cage birds. They were also exported to Europe for this same purpose; there they were known by the name "linnet," or "red linnet."

🖎·Learning the Value of Predators

I was not happy about what I saw. My neighbor had spotted the large, horned owl hanging dead, its middle toe held fast in a steel trap that was caught on a high branch of an oak tree.

The owl had managed to pull the trap loose from its original mooring and had flown off with the long chain and trap dangling from its toe. The bird was doomed to death by starvation, a premature and senseless death which, in reality, had helped to defeat the purpose of the trapper.

Slowly, legislators and responsible citizens are becoming more informed and concerned about the "balance" of nature and how a natural balance actually helps man.

Hawks and owls are being found on the protected list in more states. Already, all are on Kentucky's protected list except the Cooper's hawk, sharp-shinned hawk (not a very common bird), and the horned owl.

It is my hope that all three will be added to the list soon; although individuals among these birds will occasionally take a chick or chicken, it is not the nature of the birds to depend on man's domestic fowl for their food. Those that do are undoubtedly (and justifiably) taken by man, but I cannot see a blanket condemnation of a species as being in man's best interest.

I know of a hunting-preserve owner who annually traps all the horned owls he can. (Incidentally, his traps do not discriminate between different species of predatory birds.) He rea-

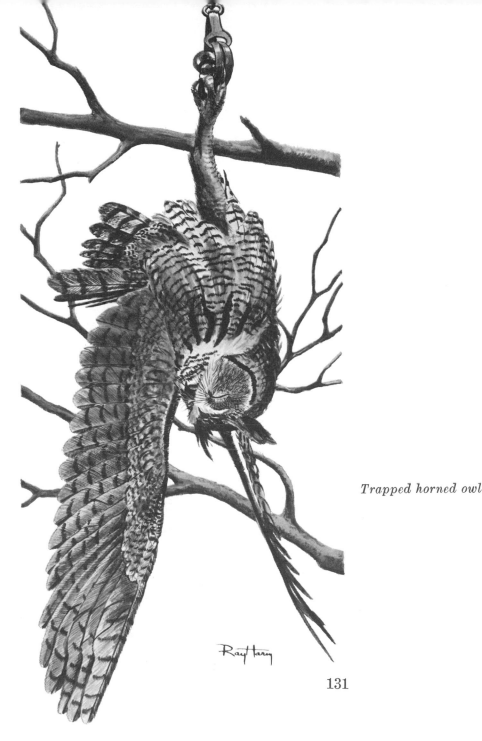

Trapped horned owl

131

sons that the owls prey upon his quail, thus reducing his income from hunters. This, he feels, justifies his trapping.

He does not reason far enough, however. As a result of his trapping of owls, he is really increasing his loss of quail. Naturalists know that ground-swelling animals such as wood rats, skunks, and snakes destroy great numbers of quail annually by eating the eggs of these birds.

When the trapper takes the owl and hawk he allows these prolific animals to multiply even more rapidly than normally. Consequently, the quail loss is far more than is caused by the predator's taking of an occasional bird. The primary diet of the owl, fox, and hawk is rodents.

Changing Country Alters Wildlife

How do you stand on the question of starlings in urban society? This gregarious bird now ranks as the second most abundant bird species in the nation. Cities are the host to these birds and supply them with everything they need to thrive. Around the turn of the century, this species was brought from Europe, and a few were released on the East Coast. They now range from coast to coast.

There is no doubt that in some areas they have become a serious problem, not only an inconvenience to man; when they mass together in the fall in enormous flocks, they can virtually strip wild or domestic trees and shrubs of their fruit.

The problem really lies in man's continuing to supply them with year-round, unlimited food and shelter. Our streets, parks, backyards, and city dumps all provide scattered or concentrated refuse to support an overpopulation of starlings. This is contrary to what would normally occur in nature's balance, for a natural area will support only a limited amount of wildlife.

Since the early days of our country there has been a gradual change from forests to cleared land. Today we have birds that are quite common to us but rarely seen by pioneers—for instance, meadowlarks (eastern), field sparrows, bobolinks, and horned larks. We have introduced species such as ring-necked pheasants, Hungarian partridges, and other "exotics" that have been in our country a comparatively short time.

Each has its own habitat, however, and one never finds a meadowlark in the woods, nor an ovenbird in the fields. Being aware of this, a naturalist knows what he is talking about when he voices concern about certain species being endangered because of man's pushing the scenery around.

At present, the country's most abundant bird is still probably the red-winged blackbird, although the starling is in close competition.

Our rarest bird is probably the everglade kite or the ivory-billed woodpecker. The latter is surely doomed to extinction because man has all but eliminated its necessary habitat. Total elimination is just a matter of time.

Our largest American bird is the trumpeter swan, with a wingspread of almost ten feet. It

Ruby-throated hummingbird

133

may weigh as much as thirty pounds. Of course, the ostrich is the largest bird in the world, although flightless.

The fastest bird is not the hummingbird, as many believe, but the swift, which attains speeds up to two hundred miles per hour in straight flight.

Hummingbirds are the smallest birds. Our ruby-throated hummingbird, although not the smallest, is only about three and one-half inches long.

ꙮ·Wild Seeds Fly, Swim, Hitchhike

Nature has provided wild seeds with just about every possible means of being transported.

The sometimes too abundant "sticktights," "cockleburs," and beggar-lice are picked up on the fur and feathers of animals, to be carried away and brushed off to grow in other places.

Grasses and wild fruits containing seeds are also eaten by animals and, unless crushed by teeth or gizzard, are not only transported intact to some distant spot but are there deposited with a liberal portion of fertilizer to insure growth!

Seeds, even as large as those of pawpaws and persimmons, are carried down mountains and hillsides by springs and creeks. Gravity helps distribute countless other seeds.

We are all familar with the puffs of milk-

134   *Pawpaws*

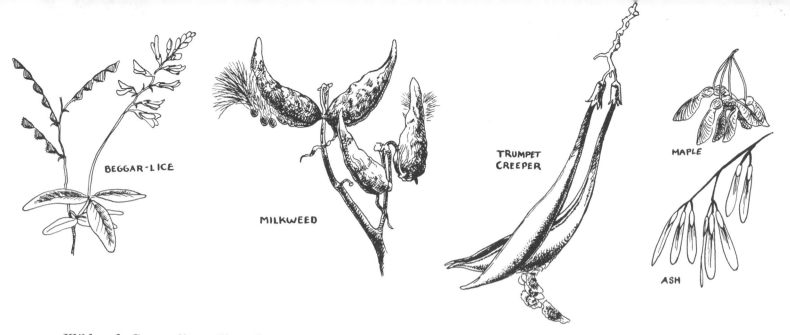

Wild seeds. Beggar lice, milkweed, trumpet creeper, maple, ash

weed and dandelion seeds carried by the summer breezes. Very interesting are tree seeds such as maple, basswood, sycamore, cottonwood, and birches, all of which produce either drifting or spinning flying seeds that are carried from the tree when they loosen.

Some types of seeds are extremely specialized in their ability to plant themselves. There is a needle grass in the West that has a seed which, by wind action, literally screws itself into the ground. The witch hazel tree has a seed pod that swells to the point of exploding its seeds as far as thirty feet away. Some seeds are planted by squirrels and other rodents when the nuts and seed pods are buried for storage, then forgotten.

As if these were not enough, plants have yet other ways of propagating. Root structures spread out, from which new growths emerge.

In face of this tremendous ability of nature to grow all forms of plant life, man is the biggest threat to their survival. I am not going to take up the arguments of nature lovers, chemical industries, and sportsmen—the eternal triangle whose three sides should be supporting rather than frequently fighting each other—but I am sure that one thing is not debatable: the world of nature can only become smaller as human population increases.

I think it was time yesterday to start thinking about conserving our wildlife areas before it is too late. Some effort has been made, but not nearly enough. Too many people just don't care.

ABOUT THE AUTHOR

The birds and the animals of Bernheim Forest, in Kentucky, have a hard time staying out of the way of Ray Harm, naturalist and wildlife painter.

Usually Harm moves quietly into the woods before dawn each day and finds a spot to sit and wait for wildlife to pass by.

"That's the time to see animals," he says. "Most people go into the woods later, but the activity is over by then."

His sketchpad is tucked inside his belt at his back, under his denim jacket, and he carries his binoculars by looping his belt through them. He wears faded levis and moccasins.

Atop a steep-backed ridge, the leaves are faintly pressed down into a path. "This is the kind of ridge that deer like," Harm says. "They can look all around them for danger.

"When you're tracking deer, you walk slow for a few feet and stop, just like they do. They make noise, too."

On an abandoned trace, he spots a cluster of bones. "I know what that is without even looking at it."

He pokes inside the bones. "Look at those persimmon seeds. Only a 'possum would likely eat that many persimmons at a time." Counting the fifty teeth in the skull confirms it to be an opossum which has more teeth than any North American mammal.

In fair weather or foul, Harm spends three to five hours early in the day in the woods. "I find it essential to get out every day to be a successful wildlife artist. I have to keep my painting and my field work equal. I've got to stay out all season so I can become a part of wildlife," he says.

If he is observing deer at a pond or birds in a nest, Harm will set up a blind and stay there for hours, day after day. In any case, he makes "field sketches" with detailed notes about color, size, and proportions.

"I paint things as they are in life," Harm said. "I try never to leave things to chance.

"I let nature do the work for me. I use the actual composition—I try to, anyhow—in my paintings."

He may spend eight or nine weeks on a painting, doing all his sketching from nature, making detailed drawings and notes on a single subject from every possible angle. He strives to make everything he draws—birds, wild flowers, trees, reptiles, amphibians, mammals, insects—structurally perfect to give authority to his art.

"Nature makes a person patient," he says. "You can't rush it."

Ray Harm does this field work in the 300-acre forested backyard of his home near Henpeck, Kentucky, where he lives with his family. The property is ten miles from the nearest town, and conveniently adjoins a 14,000-acre private wildlife preserve and refuge.

The day's work in the studio begins by 10 A.M. In the evening Harm usually works again until 8 or 9, and tries to get to bed by 9:30.

It's a strange life, for which he is miraculously suited. "I was raised in the woods, fields, plains, and desert. My interests have always been nature."

He grew up in a remote area about halfway between Elkins and Parsons, West Virginia. His father was a mountaineer and herbalist who loved wildlife, and who knew how to find food in the woods—characteristics his son has acquired.

When Ray Harm was 15 he went to work on a ranch in Nebraska and later became a rodeo performer, then went into the Navy, and eventually decided to give up the horse business for art school.

He has had a lifetime of experience and only seven years of formal schooling. In the lean years that followed art school, the coincidence of his sending a painting to a purchaser in Florida led to his present situation.

The then-president of the University of Kentucky, a house guest of the purchaser, happened to see the painting and invited Harm to present an exhibit of paintings at the university. Another guest of the purchaser, who is now the artist's sponsor, immediately commissioned him to do paintings of 20 Kentucky birds.

Today, at 40, he is Herman L. Donovan artist-in-residence at the University of Kentucky, writes and illustrates a column for the *Louisville Times,* is a contributing editor for *The Florida Naturalist* magazine and staff artist for the Kentucky Ornithological Society, has a lecture contract with the State Parks of Kentucky, and has over five years' work on advance commissions for paintings, as well as a corporation that has been formed to reproduce and distribute a full collection of his wildlife paintings in collectors' editions of one-time printings.